Advance Praise for
YOU GOTTA BE YOU

"Had I had access to the testimonies and musings found on every page of *You Gotta Be You* when I was coming of age, I may have spent more days loving myself. Brandon Kyle Goodman's words are a reminder of the power of Black Queer self-determination. *You Gotta Be You* is a meditation on Black Queer life that is full of the sharp wit, singular humor, and courageous candor that has come to define its author. Someone's life will be transformed because of Goodman's gift."

—**Darnell L. Moore, author of *No Ashes in the Fire***

"Brandon is such a beautiful example of the joy one can have when you truly embrace who you are, and that joy is contagious! The world is a brighter (and funnier) place because of their work and shows other folks that the most beautiful gift they can give to the world is to be themselves."

—**Tess Holliday, author of *The Not So Subtle Art of Being a Fat Girl***

"Brandon is a force of nature: funny, honest, messy, and real. *You Gotta Be You* showcases a level of introspection that takes most people a lifetime to achieve. There's a lesson in these pages for everyone."　　　　　　　　　　—**Nick Kroll**

"A graceful, heartening story of Brandon's journey toward finding himself. I felt like he was holding my hand the whole way through. *You Gotta Be You* is a visceral cue to cherish those who nurture your soul, and a reminder to 'borrow their eyes' in an attempt to 'see yourself the way they see you.'"

—**Colton Haynes, author of *Miss Memory Lane***

"In *You Gotta Be You* Brandon Kyle Goodman beautifully chronicles the way they've whittled away at a hunk of metal to create a skeleton key for themselves—a key to unlock their most honest self, a key to free themselves from society's oppressive expectations, a key to be themselves. Reading this book will inspire you to take a chisel to your own hunk of metal. It will dare you to see what you might unlock in yourself."

—**Dylan Marron, author of *Conversations with People Who Hate Me***

YOU GOTTA BE YOU

YOU GOTTA BE YOU

How to Embrace This Messy Life and Step Into Who You Really Are

BRANDON KYLE GOODMAN

LEGACY
LIT

BOSTON NEW YORK

Legacy Lit, an imprint of Hachette Books
Hachette Book Group
1290 Avenue of the Americas
New York, NY 10104
LegacyLitBooks.com
Twitter.com/LegacyLitBooks
Instagram.com/LegacyLitBooks

First Edition: September 2022

Grand Central Publishing is a division of Hachette Book Group, Inc. The Grand Central Publishing name and logo is a trademark of Hachette Book Group, Inc.

The publisher is not responsible for websites (or their content) that are not owned by the publisher.

The Hachette Speakers Bureau provides a wide range of authors for speaking events. To find out more, go to www.hachettespeakersbureau.com or call (866) 376-6591.

Scripture quotations are from the ESV® Bible (The Holy Bible, English Standard Version®), copyright © 2001 by Crossway Bibles, a publishing ministry of Good News Publishers. Used by permission. All rights reserved.

Library of Congress Cataloging-in-Publication Data

Names: Goodman, Brandon Kyle, author.
Title: You gotta be you : how to embrace this messy life and step into who you really are / Brandon Kyle Goodman.
Description: First edition. | New York, NY : Legacy Lit, [2022] | Summary: "From the time we're born, a litany of do's and don'ts are placed on us by our families, our communities, and society. We're required to fit into boxes based on our race, gender, sexuality, and other parts of our identities, being told by others how we should behave, who we should date, or what we should be interested in. For so many of us, those boxes begin to feel like shackles when we realize they don't fit our unique shape, yet we keep trying because we crave acceptance and validation. But is "fitting in" worth the time, energy, and suffering? Actor, writer, and activist Brandon Kyle Goodman says, Hell no it ain't! As a Black non-binary, queer person in a dark-skinned 6'1", 180-pound male body born into a religious immigrant household, Brandon knows the pain of having to hide one's true self, the work of learning to love that true self, and the freedom of finally being your true self. In You Gotta Be You, Brandon affectionately challenges you to consider, "Who would I be if society never got its hands on me?" This question set Brandon on a mission to dropkick societal shackles by unlearning all the things he was told he should be in order to step into who he really is. It required him to reexamine messy but ultimately defining moments in his life-his first time being followed in a store, navigating his mother's born-again Christian faith, and regretfully using soap as lube (yes, you read that right!)-to find the lessons that would guide him to his most authentic self. Compassionate and soulful, funny and revealing, You Gotta Be You is an unapologetic call to self-freedom. It's about turning rejection (from others and yourself) into a roadmap to self-love. It's a guide to setting boundaries and fostering self-growth. And most importantly, it's an affirmation that we are enough exactly as we are"—Provided by publisher.
Identifiers: LCCN 2022019431 | ISBN 9780306826191 (hardcover) | ISBN 9780306826221 (ebook)
Subjects: LCSH: Self-acceptance. | Self-esteem. | Self-realization. | Identity (Psychology) | Discrimination.
Classification: LCC BF575.S37 G66 2022 | DDC 158.1—dc23/eng/20220629

LC record available at https://lccn.loc.gov/2022019431

ISBNs: 978-0-3068-2619-1 (hardcover), 978-0-3068-2622-1 (ebook)

Printed in the United States of America

LSC-C

Printing 1, 2022

Dedicated to Grandma and Mommy.

"I am a human being, and thus nothing human is alien to me."

—TERENCE

Contents

Introduction xiii

1. **Being Messy Is Not Just for Mondays** 1

2. **Fem** 17

3. **The Man** 37

4. **They** 53

5. **YouOnSomeFuckShitVille** 59

6. **Author's Note: Holding Space** 77

7. **Gay Stuff** 83

8. **Author's Note: Boundaries** 103

9. **Life Is Hard. We All Deserve Help.** 109

10. **Make It Home** 129

11. **The Gorgeous Swan You Are** 145

12. **Pride and Joy** 163

13. **Three-Fifths** 183

14. **You Gotta Be You** 185

Acknowledgments 193

Introduction **Take what you need. Take what's useful. Leave the rest.**

WAS SITTING IN FRONT OF MY COMPUTER thinking about how I wanted to start this book. How I wanted to introduce myself to you. What I wanted you to learn about me and feel about me in the first few moments of reading. But, as usual, I got distracted by a notification on social media, which led to me mindlessly scrolling past different memes, reels, and photos of friends and celebrities. After a few minutes (or maybe hours—who knows!), I came across a post that stopped me in my tracks. It was Oprah (Winfrey, obvi, who else?) in a colorful sweater, sitting at the bottom of a white staircase, looking into a camera, and saying, "Give up hope that the past could have been any different."

Oowee! That's so nice, I'ma type it twice.

"Give up hope that the past could have been any different."

As I love me some Oprah, this seemed like a good writing omen, considering this book is an exploration of my past and how we all must reckon with our complicated, often painful experiences to find our most authentic selves. But before we get into that, let's talk about Mother O.

Growing up in the '90s, kids of a certain age generally came home after school to watch shows like *Power Rangers* or *My Little Pony*, but for me, *The Oprah Winfrey Show* was my obsession. I would sit in the living room with my Trinidadian grandmother every weekday at four p.m., and we would laugh, cry, scream, and revel in the glory of Harpo Studios all from the comfort of our little house in Queens.

Oprah's show was a free master class. Unlike my private school in the bougie Queens neighborhood of Jamaica Estates, Oprah educated me on the real shit. The life shit. She encouraged her viewers to believe in themselves. Showed us how to heal relationships. Taught us about persevering through tragedy. Not to mention she would fangirl over celebs as though she wasn't the biggest celebrity herself. Baby, before Beyoncé, before Brandy, I worshipped at the altar of O.

On several occasions, Oprah has told the story about an early episode of her show where her guests were members of the Ku Klux Klan. She'd hoped that with a conversation on air she could reform their white supremacist beliefs toward Black folx, but it turned out they were using her platform to recruit. After another episode later that week that left a bad taste in her mouth, Oprah called a meeting with her producers declaring that she would no longer be part of "sensationalized television" and required that every episode moving forward have an *intention*.

I love the idea of intention. To me, intention is more than just a plan—it's defining what you're pursuing, why you're pursuing it, and the desired outcome or goal of that pursuit. I think Oprah's directive resonated with me because as a Black Queer person, I've been called every name in the book.

Faggot.

Sissy.

Punk bitch.

Darky.

Nigger.

Nigger faggot.

I've been made to feel less than. I've been criticized, ostracized, and marginalized, oftentimes by people I know and love. What was their *intention*? To "toughen" me up? Make me more masculine? Guilt me into heterosexuality? Prepare me for the world's anti-Blackness? I still couldn't tell you, but after so many years of being bullied and chastised, I decided I never wanted to make anyone feel as worthless. As disposable. So I hold a personal and artistic mandate for intention in everything I do. It has been a foolproof way to honor my humanity and the humanity of others in both my life and my work.

This book is about my life, but it's also my work, so you better believe that like my live shows, my social media, or the projects I sign on to—be it writing or voicing a character on *Big Mouth*, a TV show about puberty; playing a gender-bending best friend in a family film like *Feel the Beat*; being an advocate of sexual health and wellness through my *Messy Mondays* Instagram series; or hosting podcasts about antiracism, mental health, and the Black experience—I know my intention. And I'll definitely share it with you, but this is a book, honey, so let's start with a story first, shall we?

I think I was thirteen when I was coming home from school and a group of six older kids were sitting on their stoop. They were labeled the "troublemakers" of our block because they were affiliated with some of the neighborhood's gang activity, and I would have to walk by their stoop in order to get to my house, which I was scared to do. I could have walked down another block or through the alleyway, but those paths also felt unsafe. So to pass the time I busied myself by browsing through familiar shops like the nearby Dunkin' Donuts or a local grocery store called Trade Fair. I hoped eventually the kids would go inside and I'd be able to walk home.

It took hours, but finally, after the sun had set, the older kids were nowhere in sight. I quickly made my way down the block and into my house, where I was met by my worried mother and grandmother. My mother, a petite, dark-skinned actress whose presence is far larger than her frame, yelled out in shock, "Jesus, boy, where have you been?!" My grandmother chimed in with her Trinidadian accent, "My God, child, what happened?!" This was before I got my first cell phone, so they were truly unable to locate me for hours. They examined me for any signs of distress, anything that would explain why I'd gotten home so late. But there were none. Just me. Afraid.

Their worry quickly turned to anger.

When I expressed that I was scared to walk by the house with "the troublemakers," my mother declared she was putting me in karate classes. I'd already taken judo, another martial arts practice, years prior, and hated it. To my mother, putting me back in a martial arts class was a solution, but for me it felt like a threat, partly because martial arts felt like a very masculine space, with lots of boys at school interested in the practice. Even though I couldn't have articulated it at the time, I was Queer, and hypermasculine heteronormative settings were never welcoming for a kid like me.

I think that's why I also knew I couldn't walk down the block past those older kids. I knew that I was a target to them, based on the intonation of my voice, the limpness of my wrist, and the way my hips sauntered when I walked. In my neighborhood, being a Black gay kid was seen as a weakness, and I always feared that if I stood up for myself, I'd be in a bloody situation, which is the very reason my mother wanted to put me in karate class.

Growing up, I lived in fear a lot. I knew that people around my way called me a "fag," and eventually, when I went away to boarding high school in Georgia, a "nigger." But I didn't know how to change that. I didn't know how to not be those things. A nigger faggot. By the time I reached adulthood, I'd become intimately familiar with rejection, perfectionism, depression, and conditional love, all as a result of grappling with the labels that had been placed upon me when I was a child.

There aren't many things that I *hate*. My grandmother would always remind me that "hate" was a strong word and to be careful how I use it. But I can safely say that I hate the ways in which people and society get to tell us who we are before we get to know ourselves. Most of us are working off blueprints of our lives that have been provided for us—well, really, forced on us—instead of drafting our own. What's said and what's not said, what we see and don't see...these things govern us, reinforced through the media, our communities, and our loved ones. As a result, many of us shapeshift so that we can achieve the ultimate trophies, the ABVs: Acceptance. Belonging. Validation. And in the name of the ABVs, I've often denied the most beautiful parts of myself that I'm now on a hunt to find.

*　　*　　*

I named this book *You Gotta Be You* based on the mid-'90s song "You Gotta Be" by Des'ree, which my mother used to play on repeat for me. As much as I loved that song (and still do), looking at it now, I realize it was filled with so many commands about what and who you're supposed to be. Though the sentiment (and intention) was inspirational, the number of directives is overwhelming. "You gotta be bad, you gotta be bold, you gotta be wiser." It continues with you gotta be hard, tough, stronger, cool, calm, AND you gotta stay together. I mean, bless the person who can be all these things, but I'm stressed just reading it. Not to mention the phrase "you gotta be" took on a different meaning as I began to reflect on my life and upbringing. I was constantly being told what I *gotta* be, and when I began the journey of learning how to love myself in a world that doesn't love Blackness, Queerness, or Black Queerness, it meant unlearning all those things. It meant putting the directives aside and daring to get curious by asking a very big question:

Who would I be if society never got its hands on me?

Who would I be if there wasn't a blueprint forced on me, if there wasn't a never-ending list of all the things "you gotta be"? I don't have the answer, but I feel like I've gotten closer to finding out. Closer to who I was *before* I was told who I *gotta be*.

When you're part of any marginalized group, resilience is how you survive. Or at least that's what's taught—sometimes purposefully, and sometimes it's learned by what we see. I think resilience can actually be like a knight's armor, and armor is heavy. Weighted. It impacts how you hold yourself and how you move. It also helps you survive some traumatic blows, in this case, by protecting you from feeling the depths of your pain so that you can move forward with your life. But I also think that protection, though oftentimes necessary, is what creates a barrier to knowing who you really are. I define this as the gray space, a place where multiple truths get to coexist, like how resilience can be a necessary protection while also keeping you from knowing yourself.

So, in the quest to get closer to who I was before society, community, and family got their hands on me, I'll need to lay the resilience down, reexamine hard moments of the past with my present-day eyes, and reckon with all the feelings that were never processed. I hope that in continuously doing all of that work, I'll be able to find healing. And I hope the same for you. It's in healing that you can actually discover your most authentic self—the <u>only</u> thing you gotta be.

Woof! There's so much for us to get into and that I want to share—which for me is both exciting and scary. Gray. But for now, I want to share that I hope you get the journal style of this book and feel free to embrace it and all of its lessons as your own. I've been writing in journals since the third grade, so I'm kind of an expert at it. My journaling started with poems. Oh, how I loved to pen poetry. Can you picture my skinny eight-year-old self, crouched at the bottom of the steps, scribbling away in my black-and-white notebook, musing about my deep love for the playground? Precious.

As I got older, I began writing brief musings about random topics and thoughts, be it about a particular person or about a concept. A quote from Toni Morrison reads: "Writing is really a way of thinking—not just feeling but thinking about things that are disparate, unresolved, mysterious, problematic, or just sweet." I love that, because writing has always been my way of processing the enormity of life.

As with any journal, I will share a few of my most personal stories. I hope that you'll hold them as gently as I'm trying to. In my stories, some people might seem like "villains," but as my mother used to say, "Everybody is doing the best they can with what they know and have." I do believe that everyone I talk about did the best they could, myself included. Sometimes their best held me up, and sometimes their best left a scar. This book isn't about dragging anyone through the mud or even holding anyone accountable. It's about what those encounters taught me and what I want you to learn with me. It's about how I'm using each piece—good, bad, and gray—to build the life I dreamed for myself when I was a kid. In many ways, this book is also for my younger self, presenting all the things I wish I had known or that someone would have told me.

This book will not be neat and linear, but I'll take care of you. Expect to be guided through a mix of interconnected essays, musings, quotes, and affirmations that I hope will satiate whatever curiosity you might have about my journey to "just being" while also whetting your appetite for your own exploration.

Speaking of experiences, I've already made a brief reference to my "Blackness," "Queerness," and "Black Queerness," so before we get too far, let me quickly talk about the intersections of my identity. But I don't think we can talk about "intersections" without first defining intersectionality. The word was coined by Kimberlé Crenshaw to highlight the ways in which Black and brown women experience a combination of racism and sexism that functions differently from racism alone or sexism alone. Over the years, the definition has been expanded to include other marginalized folx. In a 2017 interview with Columbia Law School, Crenshaw described intersectionality as "a lens through which you can see where power comes and collides, where it interlocks and intersects. It's not simply that there's a race problem here, a gender problem here, and a class or LGBTQ problem there. Many times that framework erases what happens to people who are subject to all of these things."

For the purposes of this book, I'm using the concept of intersectionality to examine the events of my personal life. Essentially, I'm not just Black, I'm gay. I'm not just gay, I'm nonbinary. I'm not just nonbinary, I'm Black (and so on, and so forth). As actress, host, and social media icon Ts Madison said during an interview on the popular radio show *The Breakfast Club*, "We're not Black, *then* Queer. We're Black *and* Queer at the exact same time."

That means when you're Black, sometimes your Queer sexuality prevents you from being accepted by other Black folx, as demonstrated with the "troublemakers" on my block. When you're gay, sometimes your Blackness alienates you from being welcomed by other gay folx. When you're nonbinary, sometimes your gender identity and how you express it keeps you from being acknowledged by Black folx *and* gay folx. So running questions arise: Where are you accepted? Where do you belong? Where is your existence validated? I feel the answer should be *by me*, but I can admit that hasn't often been the case.

The last thing I'll say before I share my intention is that in my twenties, I had a mentor, Ellen Barber. She's an older Jewish woman with dark hair and bright eyes magnified by her clear-framed glasses. Her spirit is sweet, warm, and fierce. The definition of a mama bear. Whenever offering nuggets of wisdom, she would say, "Take what you need. Take what's useful. Leave the rest." As I share with you these different parts of myself, I say the same thing to you: Take what you need. Take what's useful. Leave the rest.

Okay, now the moment you've been waiting for...

My intention is to get free. My intention is to liberate myself from the expectations, standards, and shackles of a society steeped in white supremacy, misogyny, homophobia, classism, and every other -phobia and -ism that barricades me from my authentic self and my most authentic existence. My intention is to revisit the experiences that have brought me to this present moment with as little judgment as possible, but with as much curiosity as I can muster. My intention is to share myself with you in hopes that if you're dancing with the pain of being rejected—or worse, you've rejected yourself— maybe my stories might be a glimmer of hope. Maybe by showing you my deepest scars, you might feel less alone in yours, and one day you, too, will use the wisdom of your experiences to make someone else feel less alone.

This book is my love letter to Black Queer folx and anyone fighting to love themselves unconditionally despite not knowing what that looks or feels like or if you're worthy of it. (Spoiler alert: You are beyond worthy. You are enough as you are. If this is the last thing you read in this book, know that YOU are enough.)

**You always have to have a relationship with hope.
In the midst of despair, you have to find the light.**

—VANESSA, MY THERAPIST

STILL LEARNING

I find myself still navigating my relationship to and with this Black Queer body.

Often viewed as a threat. Always expected to stay in line. To know its place. To exude masculinity. To entertain. To accept the leftovers. To perform according to (white) societal standards and expectations. I reject the limitations put on me, but I have to learn how to not put them on myself.

Still learning not to let others define what my identity means or what it should look like. Still learning to be comfortable with who I am even if who I am makes others uncomfortable. Still learning to quiet the voices of doubt, shame, and fear. Still learning to shake off the expectations of others. Still learning to ignore and dismantle constructs of oppression. Still learning to allow this life to be a journey, a process, an experience that's allowed to evolve, shift, and transform. Still learning about who I would be if society never got its hands on me. Still learning how to step into that. Still learning how to just exist. To just be.

Me.

1. Being Messy Is Not Just for Mondays

S O, I JUST TOLD YOU that this book won't be written in a linear way, which then raises the questions: Where do we start? How do we commence this journey together? I think we should begin with my favorite topic...sex. Oop! Somebody's bootyhole just tensed up. Breathe, baby. Ain't nobody gotta know that we're gonna chat about s-e-x. Furthermore, I'm just gonna talk about *my* experiences, though by the end, I may have you pondering your own sex life and relationship to it. But that's okay. Curiosity is fabulous.

Before we dive in, let me give you a little context. It's going to get somber for a second, so bear with me. In the summer of 2020, after watching the brutal murder of George Floyd, I made a video on Instagram called "To My White Friends." For almost ten minutes, I sat at my desk talking into a camera, telling my white friends what I needed them to know about how George's death and all the murders of unarmed Black people weigh on me and my community. At this time, my social media following on Instagram was at around 3,000 followers. I went to bed that night and woke up to almost 30,000 followers, with my video quickly climbing to a million views.

Coincidentally, I was about to begin promoting a family film on Netflix called *Feel the Beat*, starring my friend Sofia Carson. In it, I played her best friend, a flamboyant costume designer named Deco. I was to begin doing press for the movie, highlighting the importance of a Black Queer character in a film made for kids, but due to that first video going viral (and a few subsequent videos along with it), the virtual press "tour" quickly pivoted from being about the movie to being about my thoughts on racial justice. I was doing interviews and panels, making more videos, participating in Instagram live feeds, writing op-eds, and helping the Biden campaign, not to mention hosting two podcasts and getting a deal to write this book. All of this was going down while I was still writing and providing voice-overs for the Netflix adult animated series *Big Mouth* and its spin-off, *Human Resources.*

When winter finally arrived, I was beyond exhausted. Yes, physically, but more so emotionally. I had spent nearly seven months unpacking my Black Queer pain while also managing the sudden visibility and platforms where people could access me in a way I'd never experienced.

I felt trapped, like suddenly I had to be this serious person who only spoke about injustice and pain. But the reality is I love a good dick joke. I love to laugh. Correction: I love to cackle. I love delicious food, great friends, and *Real Housewives.* I wanted that to be okay, too. I wanted to be able to be a full person in my public life, and I came to realize that joy is part of my activism. It has to be. It's the only way that fighting for my life and the lives of my communities is sustainable.

So, on the Monday before Christmas 2020, I hopped on my Instagram stories and asked my followers to "tell me something good or messy." Answers began to flood in, some of them so inspiring and heartwarming, and some of them raunchy as hell. All of them joyful! I began sharing responses and recording my reactions, most of which were just me laughing. That laughter resonated with people, so I did it again the following Monday. And again, the following Monday. And the Monday after that. And thus "Messy Mondays" was born. As time went on, it morphed into a safe and inclusive space to talk about sex, relationships, kink, and even mental health. From douching to pegging to kissing to sexting, nothing is off the table. Oh, honey, we be talking about it all!

Followers dubbed me the Curator of Mess, as though we were in some kind of messy art gallery. I call them Messy Patrons. (If you're a Messy Patron reading this, hi, boo!) As time went on, Patrons began calling me Messy Mom, and honestly, teaching Patrons motherly things like how to better suck a big dick or dodge a fuckboy is the highest honor.

But moms can learn too. Creating this safe space to honor people's questions and promote pleasure and exploration inherently opened up a new level of exploration for myself and inspired introspection on my own relationship to sex.

I'm sure because of how open I am online, most people would

think I have the healthiest relationship to sex, but it's quite the opposite. I think Messy Mondays unintentionally became a way for me to heal my own sexual pain, shame, and trauma, which is tied up in my sexuality, my body, my gender identity, and my race.

I don't think I've ever admitted this, but I've never had penetrative sex with a woman. In middle school, high school, and freshman year of college, there were girls I dated, made out with, and had oral sex with, but my dick was never in a vagina. I didn't admit my love of dick and men until I was twenty-one, and even after coming out, there was still a stack of shame that I had no idea how to identify, let alone pull apart. I hadn't taken time to understand how growing up in a religious household with heterosexual Caribbean-born women who deemed homosexuality a sin contributed to my understanding of sex. I hadn't considered that I grew up in a country where representations of gay men were few and far between, where we were usually caricatures, the butt of jokes, or dying of AIDS. In what world would there *not* be shame and fear deeply laced in my sexual experiences?

I also think about how many Queer folx don't explore their sexuality with one another in high school and college like our straight counterparts do, because we're closeted. By the time we do—many of us being in our twenties, some even in our thirties or later—our romantic and sexual experiences are laced with an "immaturity" that doesn't match our age.

I'm going to break that sentence down a little more, because it's a big generalization with triggering words. Usually there's a negative connotation associated with "immature," especially with men. Like your underwear clearly has skid marks and you think everything's a joke. That's not what I mean when I say "immature" in this instance. I truly just mean this piece of our existence often isn't allowed to be explored, and by the time we begin exploring, that part of us isn't as developed in comparison to some of our straight friends.

I'll give you two examples. The first time I had sex with a guy, I was eighteen and a freshman at NYU. The guy was a musical theater major and I was just a regular theater major. We lived in the same dorm, and because of what we were studying, we ran in similar circles. At the time, I wasn't out of the closet, but he very much was. I have to admit his unapologetic gayness was so sexy to me. One Friday night, I ended up having drinks with him and a few others, not too far from our dorm. We went to a place called Asian Pub, which wasn't run by anyone Asian but also didn't card. You could eat as much edamame as you wanted while sipping Big Gulp–size mojitos and margaritas.

Culturally, the establishment was confused, but I always left extremely drunk. The night with the musical theater major was no exception. We both stumbled back to the dorm, and he asked if I wanted to come up to his room.

"Yes!" I blurted out.

We made our way to his room, and on his wall was a poster for the musical *Anything Goes*. Turns out we both played the male lead character, Billy, in our respective high school productions. There was something hot about two Billys—a straight character, by the way—tussling in this twin dorm bed together.

Finally, he asked me, "Are you a top or bottom?" I had never heard the terms and began racking my brain, trying to remember the porn I'd watched to see if the answer was buried somewhere in my subconscious. I came up short, so it was time to pivot to my "critical thinking" skills. I determined he was probably asking if I wanted to lay on my back while he was on top of me, presumably riding my dick. So, I said "bottom"! Satisfied with my answer, he pulled out a condom, and then, to my surprise, started putting it on *his* dick. Me (and my bootyhole) quickly learned that we did *not* know what "top" or "bottom" meant. But looking back, I also don't know how I would have. I was in the closet and barely knew anything about sex, let alone Queer sex.

(By the way, if you don't know, being a top or bottom has nothing to do with a position you're in, like "missionary" or "cowgirl," but rather the position you will "play" during intercourse. "Top" refers to the person who'll penetrate. "Bottom" refers to the person who'll be penetrated. Cue that big NBC shooting star that blazes across your TV screen with the words "The More You Know" underneath.)

A year after sleeping with the musical theater major, I was now a sophomore and still in the closet. After a night of lots of drinks, I found myself alone in a dorm room with a friend of mine. He made the first move, and I couldn't have been happier, because I was so attracted to him. This time I knew the difference between being a top and being a bottom, but still, with both of us not being out, we probably hadn't considered that we might be having gay sex that evening, and we were still inexperienced. He attempted to enter me, but it wasn't working. We determined we needed lube— obviously!—but we had none. He then had a bright idea. He went to the bathroom and filled his hand with...liquid soap from the dispenser. Not just any soap—that bubblegum-pink soap that can only be found in dormitories and airport bathrooms. The medical-grade soap that is not meant to do anything but burn that bacteria off your hands. I didn't even think to object. (Honestly, I was eager.) I thought it was brilliant, and I was excited to get fucked. The soap worked. It got him inside me—and then I immediately pushed him out because my hole was...ON...FIRE.

How do two nineteen-year-olds not know that SOAP IS NOT LUBE?!?! Sexual immaturity.

I wish I could say sex got better after those experiences, but sex didn't really become electric until my thirties. In fact, in my mid-thirties, I've had extraordinary, mind-blowing, otherworldly, ugly-cum-face, can't-walk-straight, left-with-a-smile type sex. Don't get me wrong. In the before times, I had good sex. Great sex, even. And of course, there's something to be said about age and experience, but that doesn't account for the residual guck I always had. The shame.

My Pink Soap friend and I actually ended up having a ton of sex (with actual lube), but because we were closeted, it was rarely in a romantic setting. Our encounters usually took place in a bathroom late at night where we knew no one would check, or in an empty school office after hours, or in one of our dorm rooms if our roommates were away. Shame. Shame. Shame.

Now add issues around race to that Queer shame. I recognize that my sexual trauma was also rooted in being raised in a society that values a certain definition of "attractiveness," which for a man was white, lean or muscular, straight, and masculine—none of which I fit into growing up. And if the definition of attractiveness did happen to expand and include Blackness, it was Denzel Washington, who I did not look, sound, or act like. Even before I came out of the closet, going to boarding high school in the South, it was very clear that if a white girl was dating me, it was looked down upon. Dangerous, even. And I was the danger. When I finally came out my junior year of college, NYU was diverse but still a PWI (Predominantly White Institution). Most of the gay spaces I had access to were white, because most of my classmates who were out were white. In those gay white spaces, guys reinforced the idea that to be with a Black person was a fetish. One evening, a white gay friend I was hanging out with at a bar told me that while I was in the bathroom, a drunk white guy approached him and said my friend had "jungle fever."

Now to that Queer shame and race shame, add body shame. I had gynecomastia growing up. It's a medical term for "man boobs," which are caused when the body produces too much estrogen, usually forming in puberty. When I was in eighth grade, we would have swim class on Monday afternoons. One day, after changing into my swim trunks and walking out to the pool, one of my male classmates looked at me with disgust, pointed to my chest, and exclaimed, "Ew! What are those?!" It was the last time I got into a pool until my thirtieth birthday.

I never verbalized that this encounter from when I was a pre-teen deeply impacted my adulthood. Shopping for clothes was a nightmare, because I wanted to prevent anyone from seeing my "man boobs," which I'd learned, very publicly, were a great offense. I was deeply self-conscious in clothes, and it only got worse when I was naked. In every sexual interaction, I feared that the guy would point at my chest and yell out, "Ew! What are those?!" When I was in my mid-twenties, I had gynecomastia surgery to have the breast tissue removed, but I still didn't feel comfortable shirtless until I turned thirty-two and had a transformative shift of feeling beautiful, which I'll discuss a little later. Still, I had an inner voice nagging me, saying I was too skinny, that I didn't have the perfect "man" body I was told to have by the media, my professional industry, my gay community, and others.

The final element we'll throw into the pot of shame is gender identity. Though I wasn't able to articulate that I'm nonbinary until after turning thirty-four, it was clearly present my whole life and something I wrestled with, especially being effeminate. Before being rejected for my race and sexuality, I was rejected for my femininity and not "acting like a boy." Everyone had a problem with it. People I knew and people I didn't know all took note of how fem I was and weren't afraid to tell me how wrong it was.

Take the Queer, race, body, and gender shame, stir it up in a pot, and serve it up on a daily basis, then tell me: In what world did I have a shot at having a healthy relationship to sex? There are countless moments and instances that I never unpacked, never processed. Since I didn't verbalize it, by default I ended up thinking I was indeed the problem. In fact, once I was out of the closet, if I wasn't dating someone, I rarely slept with the same person more than once, and 95 percent of the time, sex happened under the influence. I always had to be drunk or stoned. It was the only way to quiet the anxiety, shame, and fear that plagued me so that I could actually enjoy sex. Substances quieted the self-doubt and negative talk.

But wait, there's more.

In the fall of 2021, while on a Messy Mondays Instagram Live event with my friend comedian Rob Anderson, we were talking about topping and performance anxiety, which opened me up to talk about my own anxiety in my sexual experiences. I then revealed that I always felt like people were *doing me a favor* by sleeping with me. I had this unformulated, subconscious belief that no one actually wanted to be with me sexually because I wasn't attractive. I shared how my husband, Matthew, and I had spoken about this a few weeks prior and I'd told him that, subconsciously, I believed he had sex with me because we're married, not because he desired me.

Baby, when you hear me use the term "mental aerobics" or describe trauma as an "emotional web," I do not speak lightly. It's so complicated, the way that what we learn in our youth about our bodies, our skin, our gender expression, and our sexuality governs our adulthood because it's so deeply ingrained in us.

But I did start to question my assumptions, and I was finally able to articulate how so much of my sex was about...you guessed it...acceptance, belonging, and validation. It was about being picked. Being chosen. Desired. Wanted. If someone slept with me, I felt worthy, even if I thought they were doing me a favor. The goal became just to have sex, chasing the high of worthiness and hustling for my worth. But sex should be about pleasure... connection...fun...joy, filled with communication and a space to safely explore your kinks, desires, wants, and needs without judgment or shame. There ain't nothing inherently wrong with random hookups, but do that because it turns you on and you treasure the experience, not because you're running away from your shame or anxiety.

Now that's all well and good, and as fabulous as my little bedazzled soapbox is, how do you get from *shame* to *pleasure*? How do you get from *trauma* to *healing*? How do you begin questioning? Not just sex, but everything.

I'll tell you, but I warn you, it got messy. Did that just make some of y'all tense up? Me too. As someone who still struggles not to be a perfectionist, I hate mess. I can't function in mess, which is why I am a Marie Kondo stan. (If you don't know who that is, she's the queen of organization and you need to Google her immediately.) But in the heart, spirit, and soul, being messy is precisely what's needed to begin healing our traumas.

When I thought about building Messy Mondays on Instagram, the intention was to create a safe space to talk about the parts of our sex lives and relationships that we might not feel inclined to talk about in polite company. Being messy with one another was fun and funny because of the subject matter we were tackling, but it was also liberating and healing because of the radical honesty that came along with it. Knowing there's healing on the other side of messy made it less scary for me. Messy no longer made me want to crawl under the covers and hide, hoping that things would magically be in their place when I decided to reemerge.

In fact, because of how much healing Messy Mondays brought me and others, I was inspired to reclaim the word. I want it to be something we own boldly and continue to feel liberated by. I believe so deeply in the transformative power of being messy that I want it to be something we strive for, so I came up with a new definition. Because I'm a dork at heart, it's an acronym. Bish, I'm about to give you this TED Talk, honey! You ready?!

M.E.S.S.Y.

Make space to reflect curiously. When you're tackling a trauma or investigating a pattern of yours that you might want to shift or change, first make space to reflect. This could be in your journal, with a therapist, or on a hike. Up to you. As you reflect, do so curiously. Ask yourself the hard questions. Do you remember in writing class learning the "Five Ws"—who, what, where, when, and why? For example: *"Who* said or did that harmful thing to you?" *"What* was the thing?" *"Where* did it happen?" *"When* did it happen?" *"Why* did it happen?" The point is not to get definitive right-or-wrong answers—remember, sometimes there's a ton of gray—but to begin engaging with the pain, shame, or trauma you've been avoiding. The point is to identify the stack of shame you didn't even know needed to be identified, to begin caring for the wounds that are actively bleeding.

Easy on the judgment. As a kid, I was very rough with my toys, and I would also walk heavily around the house. *Stomp, stomp, stomp.* My mother would respond by saying, "Easy, easy, easy." It didn't mean I should stop playing or walking, it just meant I should be gentler. As you reflect curiously, you might come up against some cringey memories or some things that you regret. The natural instinct is to judge, sometimes harshly. But like our girl Adele sings, I beg you to go easy on the judgment. Can you be gentler with that judgment? Gentler with yourself in general?

Surrender the things you can't change. Once you've gone through your curious reflection with as little judgment as possible, surrender the things you can't change. Lay it down. The past is the past. Like Oprah said in that video I was telling you about,

"Give up hope that the past could have been any different." You or your loved ones probably made some mistakes, but you'll only experience suffering if your focus is on changing those things, because the reality is, you can't. I don't know who needs to hear that, but you simply can't. However, you can learn from what's come before.

Save the lessons you can move forward with. Everything that has happened to us—good, bad, right, wrong, or gray—has a lesson attached to it. In the moment, the lesson isn't always readily available, but with time, reflection, and surrender, those lessons begin to reveal themselves. Perhaps you can be better about communicating your boundaries, or maybe it's learning how to acknowledge and listen to your instincts in a relationship or new environment. Personally, I arguably never should have dated certain guys, but those relationships taught me that I need to listen to myself immediately when a red flag is raised, as opposed to making excuses and settling. Whatever the lesson, save it in your mind, body, heart, and spirit. Allow those lessons to help you do and be better in the present moment.

Your healing and growth are your birthright. This is the most important one for me. Often our identity is trapped in our pain. Who are we if we release the shame, if we lay the trauma down? It's impossible to know the answer until you've done so, but not knowing is terrifying—for some more terrifying than healing. It's why so often many people stay stuck. So I want to remind you that you're allowed to heal. And as you heal and gain more knowledge and new understanding, you're going to grow. You get to be different than you were ten years ago. A year ago. A month ago. You get to evolve. Healing and growth are your birthright. Take advantage of it.

I've spent a lot of time working through each of my M.E.S.S.Y. steps, and I will continue to use them as we foray into different areas of identity and unpack stories, moments, and traumas that have informed my experiences but thankfully haven't defined me—because healing and growth are my what?

Birthright.

I started us off with sex because it happens to be one of those places where the intersections of the various parts of identity can be pulled apart in all sorts of ways. I decided that in the same way I didn't just want "good" sex, I didn't just want a "good" life. I want an extraordinary, mind-blowing, otherworldly, ugly-cum-face, can't-walk-straight, left-with-a-smile type of life. And in many ways, I have that. Don't get it twisted: There are good days, bad days, and gray days. There are ups, downs, and all arounds. And my healing is a continual process. There are layers and levels to this shit, which, no lie, can be exhausting.

At base, choosing to be M.E.S.S.Y. led me to a path of happiness. It helped me stop waiting for others to accept me and led me to accept myself. I know now that I don't need to belong to anyone, because I belong to me. And baby, that's enough. But that didn't happen overnight. That said, we gotta start somewhere, we gotta start sometime.

Trauma can train you to always scan
for the weeds and thorns.
In healing, may you begin to notice the
blossoms in you and around you.

—DR. THEMA BRYANT

2. Fem

DURING MY FIRST YEAR OF WRITING on the show *Big Mouth*, a colleague of mine, Patti Harrison—a stunning and quirky Vietnamese American woman who's also an unbelievable comedian—began chatting with me about heels. She always had some of the best shoes and outfits in general, so I was eager to discuss. I've occasionally worn heels onstage but had yet to wear them casually while running errands like buying groceries or picking up edibles. I mean, wearing heels takes work, and I'm very flat-footed, so being held in that tippy-toe arched position for longer than an hour is unbearable. Honestly, I could only wear them onstage because the adrenaline of performance would distract me from the podiatric pain. (Mostly.) But Patti told me about this shoe line called Syro that catered toward Queer folx by carrying heels in bigger sizes, often platforms. (For my guys, gals, and sibs who've yet to try on heels, platforms are far easier to walk in, because you have more support.)

When I looked at Syro's website, I saw all these heels that literally left my mouth agape, and the models posing in these iconic gems were all male-presenting. There was something so captivating about the images, the blatant disregard for the binary of gendered fashion wrapping me in liberating tingles. I marveled at the courage it would take to be a man in heels, not for a stage show but in everyday life.

There was a particular pair of heels I fell in love with, made of a fabric reminiscent of the Burberry check print. I looked at the shoes for days, debating if I should purchase them. Previous purchases were always for a show, always for a character, not simply for daily life. After a week I said, "Fuck it," and I went online to buy them. To my devastation, they were already sold out. I was crushed, not because they were sold out but because I'd waited. My debate over buying the heels wasn't about money or practicality; I fretted about what others would think of me.

The labels placed on me from childhood still lingered.

Faggot.

Sissy.

Punk bitch.

Would strangers be as in awe of me as I was of those models, or would they think that I was looking for attention?

What's important to note is that my friends and chosen family would have LOVED those heels. I would have walked into brunch and been met with cheers and applause. "Yaaas, Brandon!" "Okay, bitch, we see you!" "You better serve!" My tribe is incredible like that. So really, I allowed people I *don't even know* to influence my decision.

A few months after I missed the opportunity to get those Burberry-inspired heels, I was in Toronto filming the movie *Feel the Beat.* My character, Deco, arguably filled the common position that a lot of Queer characters serve in movies—namely, "gay best friend" to the protagonist. I despise playing two-dimensional tropes that allow a studio or network to check off their "diversity box." The worst is when a movie or show will try and get a "two for one" where a character is both Queer and of color—the magical Queer negro. That part usually consists of the character saying something "sassy" while doing a makeover, and once they've completed their task, they disappear. But I agreed to this particular role because the director, Elissa Down, was adamant that this movie wouldn't present the same old tired tropes, that the project would be truly inclusive in terms of the cast. Most importantly, Elissa believed an unapologetically Queer character in a family film was long overdue. (Note: This was before any of the gay holiday films now gracing our TVs or Gonzo wearing a princess dress on *Muppet Babies*, so I couldn't argue. I didn't want to argue. I wanted to be part of that change.)

True to her word, Elissa had so many conversations with me about Deco—who he is, where he comes from, and how all of that influences his boastful style. It was during my second or third fitting at the production office that it was decided Deco would arrive in the small rural town where most of the film takes place wearing a custom leather kilt and Gucci army boots. I was in the dressing room, which was actually an empty office with one of those full-length hanging door mirrors you get for your dorm room, harsh overhead fluorescent lighting, racks filled with clothes, and a plethora of boots, sneakers, and a couple heels lined up against one of the walls. As I stood there in that leather kilt, I clocked that Deco had the same courage, fortitude, and ideologies as the models I'd seen on the Syro website months before. I opened the door to show the costume designer, her assistant, and Elissa the outfit. They were elated by it, particularly Elissa, because she was the one who'd requested the kilt.

Almost in tears, I soon pulled Elissa aside to a little corner and shared with her my realization that Deco is who I would be if I hadn't been made to feel ashamed of my flamboyance and femininity growing up.

I couldn't have been older than eight or nine when I was wearing my hair in locs just like my mother. But mine weren't as long yet. They were more like an afro with twists. I loved having hair like my mom's, and the idea of one day growing my locs out until they were cascading down my back like hers was exhilarating.

At the time that I was rocking my new hair, my mother started dating a guy who we'll call Brooklyn, which is where he lived. Brooklyn also had long locs, and he was a vision. Tall. Dark. Masculine. In addition to his good looks, he was also pretty gentle with me, which ostensibly made him a decent suitor for my mom; though, in truth, we never quite bonded.

I could tell things were getting serious between my mother and Brooklyn when we were invited to a function hosted by his family. A *holiday* function. Though I knew they liked each other and their relationship was growing, I was too young to understand just how big a deal it was to introduce your family to a girlfriend *and* her son at a holiday event. That said, at first I didn't want to go. I was always a homebody. Creature of habit. I didn't love new places or meeting new people. But I loved being around my mother, so by that alone I was persuaded to attend. (Also, I didn't know if I had a choice.)

Now, this might be a gross generalization, but when you attend a Black family gathering, you have to know that you ain't gon' eat right away. We say arrive at five, knowing you won't get there till seven, and even then, we're still putting things in the oven. So that extra time waiting for dinner is spent catching up on the family gossip or watching TV. The adults might be sprawled out through-out the house while the kids gather in a designated area. Being that my mother and I were visitors at this gathering, we had to do a little extra work to fit in.

Over music and dinner-prep commotion, my mother intro-duced me to a group of adults, including the family's patriarch. I think he might have been Brooklyn's grandfather, or maybe his great-uncle. He had brown skin, glasses, and a rounder physique. It was evident from a nearby walker that he wasn't very mobile. But what he lacked in movement he made up for in a boisterous voice that rang through the house. He took up space in a way that felt like it was his right, a right that everyone around surrendered to him. In my house, women were the ones who ran things, so the brashness of this loud patriarch was unsettling. I politely greeted him and then went to the kids' area.

New kids always brought me pause, especially if they were boys. I didn't know it then, but boys could smell my Queerness, and let's just say most of them didn't love it. At the time, I was unaware that femininity expressed by a male wasn't of value in the world. In fact, femininity was an unspoken sin. So when my "heathen" ass entered a room, boys were on alert. They were watching, con-cerned, exuding an unease that I didn't understand how to navi-gate. The dynamic was no different with the boys at this holiday gathering, so I forced myself to pay attention to the video games they played while my mother did her best to impress Brooklyn's family.

We were there for what felt like hours before dinner was served. When it was ready, I joined my mother in the dining room. The patriarch was already seated at the head of the table. I just kind of watched him, which was what I always did in new situations. My mom would always say I was quiet because I was "shy"; now, knowing that I'm Queer, I believe I was trying to make sure I was safe before I spoke. I definitely didn't feel safe with this patriarch, but I had my mom.

We sat down for dinner, and she said something to me like, "Hand me that fork, Brandon."

As I reached over, the patriarch declared loudly at the other end of the table, "That's a boy?!" He cackled. "I thought *that* was a girl! The whole time I thought *that* was a girl!" He kept laughing.

Thankfully, nobody else did. Brooklyn tried to step in and get him to stop laughing and move on with a stern "Okay," but the patriarch was stubborn, and beyond that, nobody really advocated for me. So he continued to laugh and marvel at the fact that I was *not* a girl.

I froze.

I don't remember the rest of the dinner or if he ever stopped laughing.

The next day I asked my mom if I could cut my hair off. She obliged and took me to the barber.

It's one of the first moments I can recall changing who I was or giving up something I loved in direct correlation to someone who shamed me. He shamed me for my voice and my mannerisms, which I felt I had little control over. But I had control over my hair, and perhaps shaving it off would prevent someone from mistaking me for a girl again.

What strikes me now is that I never thought there was anything wrong with my voice or my mannerisms. I was *told* there was something wrong, and isn't that how it always works? We are who we are. We like what we like and perform the way we perform. And then someone on the playground, or in our home, or at a holiday gathering tells you there's a problem with how you act. They don't just tell you, they mock you. They tease you. They beat you. They hurt you. And so you make a silent pledge that you won't give people ammunition to hurt you. You change. You shove yourself back into the box society set up for you. You bury yourself under inhibitions. You suffocate your desires. You tread lightly through a social minefield.

You lose yourself.

A tragedy.

I think losing touch with who you are and replacing it with who others say you should be can be one of the greatest tragedies of being a human. Suddenly you look up and the life you're leading doesn't belong to you. It's all based in fear, ABVs, and trauma instead of joy, freedom, and liberation.

After that evening, I spent every single day trying to speak in a lower octave, always satisfied when I'd pick up the phone and the person didn't assume that I was my mother or grandmother. I practiced walking with less of a swish and more of the "Black man limp" that I saw in hip-hop music videos. I kept my hands off my hips, smiled less, and tried to get rid of upward inflections in my voice.

My family never said anything about my shift. Perhaps they noticed and didn't say anything because they thought it was a good shift. Or perhaps they didn't notice because I wasn't as good at portraying masculinity as I tried to be. Either way, I put in a lot of effort, and finally, in my teenage years, with a little fuzz on my upper lip and puberty gracing my vocal cords, someone meeting me for the first time would think I was straight. It lasted all of five minutes before I'd get comfortable with the person and my smile would creep back in, my wrist would go soft, and my cadence would sound like my mother's.

I was vicious with myself, desperately trying to change. Then my eighth-grade English teacher announced we'd be performing a spoof of *Romeo and Juliet* for the school, and I would play Romeo. My mother, the fashion diva, outfitted me in one of her long black coats, which she cinched with this outrageous belt consisting of a series of big metal spirals linked together. It was topped off with a beret. Yes, a *beret*, bish! Like a French chapeau, honey. Listen, you couldn't tell me that I wasn't gorgeous. I was serving a LEWK!

And did the kids whisper in the audience about how gay I was? Absolutely. I watched some of the older boys in the back of the audience literally huddle, point, and laugh when I said a line. But I also saw a lot of faces genuinely bright and excited by what I was doing. I focused on them and the fact that I was playing *the* Romeo Montague. And since it was a spoof, it didn't have to be the traditional masculine love icon that the world knew. I didn't have to emulate the sensual masculinity of Leonardo DiCaprio. In fact, my femininity allowed a tragic play to be funny, which was the point of the spoof. Whoever was laughing at me didn't matter, because so many were laughing with me. I was in control of the narrative. I was in on the joke. I was funny.

Although up until this point I'd wanted to be a teacher or college professor, playing Romeo changed that. I'm also realizing now that the decision of my eighth-grade English teacher, Ms. Robbins, a Black woman, to cast me, a fem Black boy, as Romeo was probably on purpose. There were so many "boy-boys" in my class, but she picked me because, effeminate or not, I was a good performer. That moment planted in me the seed of the notion that neither my race nor my mannerisms should keep me from pursuing what I wanted. It also made me feel valued. Unlike the patriarch at dinner or kids on the playground, Ms. Robbins gave me the opportunity to excel and be an integral part of a big production, and there's nothing quite like feeling necessary.

After that performance, the theater and acting ended up becoming my safe place.

In high school, I would continue to chase the high that came from being onstage, and my drama teacher, Mrs. Ortega, was happy to aid. She cast me in mostly lead roles throughout my four years, picking plays that fit me like a glove. I portrayed Tom in *The Glass Menagerie*, Jack/Ernest in *The Importance of Being Earnest* (both by gay playwrights), and, during my senior year, the titular role in a deconstructed version of *Othello*. She chose works where my demeanor, personality, and femininity were a gift. I began to master how to use this side of myself to make a joke land or make a monologue impactful. I learned how to draw out my masculinity—from all the pretending in my middle school years—and allow masc and fem energy to dance with each other in a harmony that produced layered performances. Yes, honey, I know it was high school, but back then you couldn't tell me that I wasn't deserving of a Tony!

Theater was where I met other fem boys looking to escape the sharp claws of masculinity, all of us searching for a place where we would be valued for who we were. We were too afraid to acknowledge it, but we were each other's family. The straight kids may have looked down on us and certainly talked shit, but we had each other, so the words didn't sting as much.

Mrs. Ortega also made the pain manageable. She used to look at me as though I were the most special student who'd ever crossed her doors. Even though we never talked about my sexuality, she, like Ms. Robbins, saw me before I saw myself. And when she saw me, she didn't see something that needed fixing. She didn't see something that needed changing. She saw me whole. She treated me with a type of respect I didn't even know I deserved. With her, my femininity wasn't a hindrance or an obstacle. Every time I was with her, in rehearsal or onstage, I felt valued. I never wanted to leave our little black box theater, because the real world, our campus—well, it sucked.

Gradually, I started to hold on to that feeling of value from doing theater and carried it with me through my day. I created a goal. I wanted to go to college and study acting and become a big TV star. Accomplishing the goal was actually irrelevant; it was having something to work toward that was important. I spent less time worrying about my femininity and more time snatching them regional drama competition trophies, okurrr!

I did eventually achieve that first goal when I got into Tisch School of the Arts at NYU. Attending school, unfortunately, did nothing to distract me from my femininity. If anything, I was more aware of it than ever.

When I was young, my femininity was connected to my "boyhood." I wasn't viewed as having sexuality then, so I didn't get labeled as gay until sixth grade. (At least not to my face.) That was the turning point. From that moment on for me, femininity became synonymous with my sexual orientation, but I had yet to give myself time or space to reckon with whether or not I actually was gay. Honestly, I didn't want the time, because as far as I could tell, being gay appeared to come with some negative, even dangerous consequences.

But now, being at theater school increased the pressure for me to address my sexuality. There were fem boys everywhere. Unlike in high school, where the group of us who were fem hadn't identified as gay, at Tisch most of the fem boys were out as fuck. And if you were fem and not out, everyone assumed it was just a matter of time—"gay by May," as they would say at the start of every school year.

Needless to say, my dynamic with this college crop of fem boys was different from what I'd experienced in high school. It didn't feel like I was part of a safe unit. My femininity, which had once signaled to other fem boys in high school a sense of similarity and belonging, now signaled to these college gays that I had a "secret," a secret I wasn't ready to admit to myself, let alone them.

Yet in the midst of this label pressure cooker, I met my college best friend, a cis(gender), het(erosexual) white guy named Mycah. He was two years older than me but transferred to NYU my freshman year, which ended up putting us in the same drama classes. Mycah was the definition of "manly." Dark hair, gorgeous smile, baritone voice...muthafucka was smooth. I can honestly say I was never attracted to him sexually, but I was attracted to his sense of humor, warmth, and confidence. We met on the first day of orientation and clicked instantly. Talk about a duo who could go from cracking jokes for an hour straight to crying while watching videos of Luther Vandross or Jennifer Holliday singing live, to making a late-night run for McFlurrys and fries. He became like a big brother, and through it all Mycah never questioned me about my femininity or sexuality. It didn't matter to him, just like it didn't matter to Mrs. Ortega or Ms. Robbins.

Unfortunately, it still mattered to me. I couldn't escape the claws of acceptance, belonging, and validation. I couldn't escape wanting to be like the other cis-het masculine boys, not even by doing what I loved the most in the world, theater. I was hyper-aware of my feminine expressiveness. I was so hyperaware that even though I had a few people who accepted me and didn't need me to label myself, I still didn't see myself as "normal." And I knew that some people, especially gay boys, thought my femininity was a clear indication that I was gay.

Today, I look back and think to myself, *If there were so many fem gay boys around, why not just come out?* Well, most of the openly gay boys were white. Why is that important? Because we rarely acknowledge just how deep homophobia can be in the Black community. And culturally, in the Black community, even the liberal parts, generally homophobia still has a tight hold on us, because generally Christianity has a tighter hold. Nothing wrong with religion (which I will definitely discuss in later chapters), but we can acknowledge that often the Bible gets used to justify homophobia. If you grow up with that, as I did, it makes the reckoning a little more nuanced and complicated.

Now, yes, there are homophobic, Bible-slinging white folx for sure, but there are also plenty of white folx and white spaces that aren't homophobic. However, just because they're not homophobic doesn't exempt them from being racist or having biases (conscious or unconscious) against Black and brown folx, or other POC. Which means that a white gay boy might move to New York City, go to school in the Village (the notoriously Queer neighborhood where NYU is situated), and feel safe coming out, but a Black boy still might not, because even the gay spaces, which are mostly occupied by white folx, may not be safe. Often aren't.

Why aren't they safe? Apart from the racism and bias that can and do exist in those spaces, Black and brown Queer culture often gets co-opted as gay culture, which means white gay men tend to be the faces of our phrases, style, and demeanor. They tend to get credit, recognition, and clout without ever acknowledging or protecting the source of their expressions.

In school, I might not have been able to articulate it, but somewhere inside, I knew the white gay boys and I had different lived experiences. Different stakes. Different risks. Sure, some things might align, but enough didn't. With white gay boys, there seemed to be an unspoken expectation that I would need to be a certain kind of gay to fit in. I would need to perform and be even more fem than I was. Sassier, maybe even bringing an extreme version of my Black gayness to their spaces, which they could then take and emulate in their white-only spaces. It's a dark, cynical perspective, but I've seen it happen before. College is funny like that, with people trying on different personalities as they find themselves and navigate their insecurities around who they are. But there are some white gay boys who were square as fuck when they first arrived, and then after a little while you'd hear them speak and think, *Why do they sound Black all of a sudden?!*

All that is to say, I was in no rush to figure this shit out. I would continue doing my best to remember to butch myself up around new folx, occasionally drop the name of a girl I'd claim to have a crush on, and distract myself with monologues, scenes, and homework. I'd been doing it for years.

What was different from high school is that now I had Mycah. Unlike Mrs. Ortega and Ms. Robbins, who were teachers with built-in boundaries, Mycah was my actual best friend. And not only did Mycah value me, he also understood me. It was the first time that I felt understood by a *man*, fully accepted and protected in private and in public. I hadn't realized how much I needed that. I also saw how loving he was to the gay boys who were out. I think subconsciously that allowed me to drop my guard more and more around him. Subconsciously, I wasn't afraid of being rejected, and with my guard down came moments where I could feel the things I'd been running from.

What is this femininity?

Why am I like this?

Am I gay? Bisexual?

The beautiful thing is, I didn't have to answer those questions to feel my worth, because I felt loved. Here's the thing about the ABVs (acceptance, belonging, validation): Though I think the goal is for those things to come from within, sometimes you need them from others to help you get there. I had that from Mycah. I needed that, wanted it. And that's what got me to where I am today, with my ABVs coming from within. But never undervalue the power of a bridge. You can't get from point A to V without it.

A few months into my freshman year, I began quietly exploring sexually with a few guys, while also still hooking up with girls. The questions continued to build and mount. The denial was harder to stomach. The story I was telling myself was getting more challenging to believe, and I use the word "story" instead of "lie" purposely, because along with the denial was a desperate hope that I could shake this "gay thing" off.

Sophomore year, Mycah and I were now roommates, and during my second semester I was "hanging out" with a guy we can call Smith. He was special, because he also didn't care about me labeling myself. "If we become official, we can talk about how you identify then," he said.

One morning—and the dates and details have gotten a little fuzzy, so bear with me—I woke up to see Mycah had already headed to class. I was also supposed to be in class, but I couldn't get up. My body felt extremely heavy and weighed down. I could barely lift my legs to get out of bed. After what felt like an hour, but perhaps was a matter of minutes, I did get up. I then proceeded to slump around our dorm room aimlessly for hours, missing more than one class that morning. I hadn't informed anyone where I was or that I'd be late. I wasn't sure what I was going to do.

The perfectionist in me was spiraling, because I never missed a class, let alone three. After a couple hours, I finally managed to put clothes on, get myself on a subway, and make my way to class.

When I somberly walked into the acting studio, the halls were empty, because everyone was in class. But then my voice teacher, Katie Bull, emerged from the break room. Katie was an eccentric white woman with long hair down to her hip bones, a lot of jewelry, and a very hippie spirit. She was gentle and always emotionally attuned to her students. I'd missed her class that morning.

Katie looked up at the door and locked eyes with me. Her face immediately filled with concern, as my usual disposition was cheerful and energetic.

"Honey, are you okay?" she said.

I opened my mouth to try and say something but couldn't formulate the words. But Katie knew, her maternal instincts buzzing. She knew that I was on the verge of coming out. She rushed toward me, embraced me, and walked me to the program director's office. I think she wanted me to get excused for the day, which is exactly what ended up happening.

I wish I remember who I came out to afterward, along with the hows or whens of the entire affair. I truly, truly don't recall how I told any of my friends, including Mycah, though I'm certain he was the first friend I told.

I actually decided to text Mycah as I was writing this to see if he remembered how or when I came out to him. He called me back and let me tell you—there's a reason I don't remember how I told him. As Mycah recalls, I was hanging with Smith one weekend night and I drunkenly dialed him. He picked up and I slurred into the phone, "Hey! Hey! I have something to tell you, where you at?" He told me his location, a Thai restaurant our friends usually congregated at on Third Avenue in the East Village. I arrived with Smith by my side, and as Mycah describes it, I was "barely able to stand." In the retelling of this story, Mycah assured me that he was also drunk, I was just... drunker. As I wobbled in front of him at this Thai restaurant, he asked me what I had to tell him, and I blurted out, "Hey! I'm bisexual!"

I first came out as bisexual because part of me thought I was still attracted to women sexually, as most of my sexual experiences had been with my female classmates. But I mainly said it because I thought it would still tether me to the heterosexual world, providing a sliver of those ABVs. I do think it's important to note that in 2007, we weren't having the thoughtful conversations around bisexuality that we are now. People often joked that bisexuality was "just a bridge to being gay."

So let's enter the gray for a moment. I can't qualify whether that tactic is right or wrong, because I think many of us who wrestle with our Queer labels, whether it's sexual orientation or gender identity, may claim one thing and then, as time goes on, claim something else based on a deeper feeling of comfort. We're often in survival mode, after all. But I also want to make sure to verbalize that being bisexual is a sexual orientation that deserves to be respected and held sacred as its own identity, and someone who identifies as bisexual should never be viewed as being confused, "greedy," or on a "bridge to being gay."

So I declared to Mycah, "Hey! I'm bisexual!"

"That's great, B," he responded, and then Smith and I left.

I cackled at Mycah's recollection of the events, because it sounds so like me. In college, I was always shit-faced on the weekends. Obvi I learned that alcohol dropped my inhibitions and gave me something to blame my "gay urges" on before coming out. And now I was using it to share really important information about myself with the people I was closest to, because I didn't know how to do vulnerability yet.

I fear asking my other friends how I came out to them, so instead I will take a page out of Carrie Bradshaw's writing style and say, "And just like that…I was out." Ta-da! Certainly, I wasn't in the clear from the shame, anxiety, and other emotions that would come with taking on this label, but I was out. A step closer to healing.

I believe that I was loved out of the closet. I think it began with Ms. Robbins and continued with Mrs. Ortega, and then with

Mycah and the tight group of friends I made at NYU. I believe I felt enough safety and affirmation from my friends that I trusted nothing would change in my relationships with them. Once I was able to trust that in my heart, my body could no longer hold the secret. It was quite literally weighing me down.

It's hard to love yourself when the world tells you that because of how you look or behave or dress, you're not good enough. It's hard as a child, teenager, or adult to stand up against the masses and scream, "FUCK YOU, I'M BEAUTIFUL AS I AM!" But hopefully you run into a few angels along the way. Hopefully you run into somebody who sees you, whole. If you do, hold on to them for as long as time allows, and every now and again, borrow their eyes. Dare to see yourself the way they see you. Dare, if even for a second, to believe in yourself the way they believe in you. Find your safe space. In the age of social media and the internet, there are safe spaces out there. There are people who also have a swish in their hips and sound more like their mama than their dad. As much as it might feel like it, you're not the only one struggling with those feelings of inadequacy. Find your safe space.

Sometimes you gotta get scrappy. Sometimes your angels will come in the form of a TV show, book, song, or podcast. Find whatever affirms your beautiful existence. You get one life. Are you gon' live it for you or a toxic patriarch sitting at the head of a table you don't even want to be at? Are you gon' live it for you or a bunch of classmates you don't even know preoccupied with their own insecurities?

In the middle of my filming schedule for *Feel the Beat*, I had a day off, and as I was lying on my bed, fully inspired by Deco, I decided to hop on the Syro website again. The first set of heels that came up were these metallic silver platforms with a 5.5-inch heel. They were otherworldly. Just fabulous. I felt those same liberating tingles hugging me again, but this time, I didn't debate. I didn't worry about what others might think. I took my own advice, called on the love of all my angels, dared to honor my existence, and purchased them.

Take note of the liberating tingles in your own life, because they're trying to lead you to freedom.

> *If you do not bring forth what is within you,*
> *what is within you will destroy you.*
>
> —GOSPEL OF THOMAS

3. The Man

OR MY THIRTY-THIRD BIRTHDAY, I'd planned this fabulous trip to Las Vegas, staying in a suite at one of those fancy hotels with my husband and two of my friends. I bought us tickets to *RuPaul's Drag Race Live!*, and we were also planning on seeing Lady Gaga. But in March, there was talk about this virus that was spreading and had made its way to Los Angeles. Within a week of that news, the city was shut down due to COVID-19. We thought we'd be in lockdown for two weeks—plenty of time before my Vegas b-day in May. As you can guess, I didn't get to Vegas. Instead, I spent my birthday at home on the couch, eating my husband's famous lasagna and watching *Destiny's Child: Live in Atlanta* on YouTube. It was a good time, but not Vegas.

A few weeks after that birthday dinner, I found myself in the bathroom looking in the mirror, weeping. Birthdays have a tendency to naturally cause us to reflect. After the thrill of a party or celebration wears off, I tend to question what I've done with my life so far and what I want to do. Who I am and who I want to be. Sometimes there's satisfaction at the answers, sometimes there's judgment, sometimes there's that reckoning in the gray. This year was a reckoning like no other. My "who am I?" reckoning was coupled with a desire to learn more about my Queer community. I'd made all these videos and posts asking white people to learn about and honor Blackness. To be curious about identities and experiences that are not their own, citing that that's how they could do and be better in the fight for Black lives. In that request, I realized that there were experiences in the Queer community that I had never considered learning about. I'm a firm believer in practicing what you preach, so I got curious and began devouring videos and articles about gender identity, which included the nonbinary community. Immediately I related to the feelings and experiences of these nonbinary vloggers, influencers, activists, and content creators. With each video I watched, I felt myself becoming increasingly overwhelmed with emotion—a mix of fear, relief, intrigue, and confusion. Gray. My breathing began to shorten as my heart was beating faster. I raced to the bathroom feeling like I needed to scream, but instead I cried. That ugly cry, honey. That queen Viola Davis cry, with snot and tears mixing together on my face. Taken aback by my own reaction, I called on my meditation skills and focused on breathing. Inhale. Exhale. After a few rounds of breaths, my body began to feel a bit calmer.

Finally, after ten minutes or so, I emerged from the bathroom, a few tears still trickling down my face, and my dog, Korey, who sometimes fulfills his function as an emotional support animal (truly only when he feels like it), started licking them off my face. My husband walked into the living room, rightfully concerned, and asked me what was wrong, perhaps expecting a family emergency or slightly-older-than-quarter-life crisis.

"I think I'm nonbinary," I said.

With a sigh of relief, he smiled, looked at me lovingly, and said, "That's great." I was thankful for his warm reception and not surprised by it, as he's an incredibly sensitive person, but I wasn't sure it was all so "great."

When I was younger, like five or six years old, I loved putting my *101 Dalmatians* towel on my head and pretending I had a twin sister named "Tana." I don't know where the name came from, but Tana was a superstar. I mean long hair, tight waist, and attitude for days. No one in my house thought much of Tana, considering that, as an actress, my mother often played both male and female characters in her one-woman show.

Occasionally, in the peak of having fun, dressed up as Tana, I would ask myself, "Do I want to be a girl?" I asked myself that about a dozen times in elementary school, but the answer was always the same: If I woke up as a girl, I'd be cool with it, and if I stayed a boy, I'd also be cool with it. I didn't have a strong yearning to be either gender, I just liked dressing up and playing pretend. My favorite thing to pretend to be was a teacher, a career I had every intention of pursuing as a grown-up before I fell in love with acting. Sometimes I'd pretend I was "Mr. Brandon," and other times I'd pretend "Miss Tana" was a substitute teacher for my class. Whom I chose to be really just depended on my mood.

Though I seemed to be apathetic to my boyhood, everyone around me took pride in it. I was an only child and the only boy in my house. I was raised by a trifecta of equally powerful Black women—my mother, my grandmother, and one of my godmothers—and they joyfully doted over me like I was a little prince. But by the time I was in third grade, I'd been given a new title: "the man of the house."

It was strange to me when they started saying that. "You're the man of the house." What did that mean exactly? Sometimes if we ate dinner in the dining room instead of at the circular table in our kitchen nook, they'd have me sit at the head of the table opposite my grandmother, the matriarch of the house. Is that what it meant? It determined where you sat at the dinner table? I knew from television that the fathers on sitcoms often strutted in saying, "I'm the man of this house" and then demanded the big piece of chicken. I love chicken, so I wouldn't have minded that perk. But something still felt off. The pattern I saw around "the man of the house" was that the title always went to husbands and fathers, so I couldn't understand how I'd been given this position. I wasn't upset about it per se, but the title still felt pretty daunting.

My own father wasn't around, so I didn't have this idea that men were great. My mother, grandmother, and godmother never bad-mouthed men (or my biological father), but his absence was still something to reckon with. I didn't want to be him, nor did I want to take over his duties. I just wanted to run around the house with a towel on my head. And I was still allowed to do that, but each year I got older, there was more emphasis on my manhood, even with my obvious femininity. And I tried to play by the masculinity handbook as best I could. But then when you add "Black" to that "man"—I mean, the description is often associated with being the most masculine, hardened, no-emotion-showing vessel walking on two legs. My Queer femininity wouldn't allow me to live up to that even if I tried.

But I still tried.

I had serious impostor syndrome. I always felt like I was a fraud, bad at being "a man." And other kids never failed to remind me that they thought the same with their relentless taunts of "You're a sissy!" But I also didn't think I was a girl. So what was I?

After years of never quite feeling the word "man" applied to me, I graduated college and moved out of the house. I was living in the city, had a job, and was having lots of sex. Men love sex, so I thought, *That's manly, right?* Maybe I actually could be this "man" that everyone spoke of. But there was always a quiet tinge of "Meh." Perhaps I was just a "guy." A gay guy.

Shortly after college, I joined a musical sketch comedy group called Political Subversities, made up of about fifteen of us from NYU. Every week, we put on a new show of around forty songs and sketches that we wrote, composed, choreographed, rehearsed, and performed about what was happening in politics and pop culture that week. I ended up creating a popular character named Latrell Lavene Lebron Lucious Lacrosse Latavier Lactaid Jackson, who was a talk show host. The character, at first glance, was easy to write off because of his flamboyance and manner of speech, but if you actually listened, he was smart as fuck. It was a way for me to take all the things I had been made to feel ashamed of—my Blackness, gayness, fem-ness—and infuse them with power.

I ended up taking the character and writing these hour-long *Latrell* shows that I performed all around New York and LA. Latrell did identify as a man, but more than that, he was just Latrell. He had a beard, and he wore makeup, fabulous tights, and jewels for days, alternating between boots, sneakers, and heels.

I didn't realize it when I created him, but I was reckoning with my own gender identity. I know that I am in a male body and generally have a male experience, specifically a Black gay male experience. And I'm proud to be seen as a Black gay man and represent Black gay men. But there's this underlying pull that's been there since the days of playing school in my bedroom and choosing to be Mr. Brandon or Miss Tana. The days of being apathetic to boyhood or girlhood. Having a lack of enthusiasm or interest in whether or not I was a boy or girl.

As I mentioned earlier, in the summer of 2020, when we were all locked away as we battled coronavirus and racism, I started learning more about my Queer community. The L, the G, the B, the T, the Q, the I, the A... I wanted to fight for my Black gay community, but I also wanted to be able to fight for trans people, asexual people, bisexual people—everybody. To do that, I would need to learn. I would need to read. I would need to engage with their experiences the same way I was asking white and non-Black people on social media to engage with my experience as a Black gay man so that we could fight a system that continues to oppress so many. I want to share some of what I learned in that research about myself and nonbinary folx, but first let's take a moment to discuss some important definitions and distinctions so that we can dive deeper into this conversation. If this is new territory for you, I ask that you read the lines below gently and as many times as you need so that you can hold space for what I'll later share.

Sex is a label—male or female—that you're assigned by a doctor at birth based on the genitals you're born with and the chromosomes you have. It goes on your birth certificate.

—PLANNED PARENTHOOD

(Note that some people are **intersex,** meaning their genitals and/or chromosomes aren't typically male or female. For example, instead of having the usual XX or XY chromosomes, someone might be born with XXY chromosomes.)

> **Gender** refers to the characteristics of women, men, girls and boys that are socially constructed. This includes norms, behaviors and roles associated with being a woman, man, girl or boy, as well as relationships with each other.
>
> —WORLD HEALTH ORGANIZATION (WHO)

As a society, we usually treat an individual's biological sex and their gender as the same thing, but they're not. Writer and YouTuber Jessie Gender explains, "Many people feel perfectly comfortable with their assigned gender based on biological sex. These people are considered cisgender...When a person's biological sex does not line up to their gender identity they're considered transgender."

And just because someone identifies as a certain gender doesn't mean they'll express that gender through the arbitrary norms dictated by society. For example, a cisgender man wearing dresses—which brings us to gender expression:

> The way in which a person expresses their gender identity, typically through their appearance, dress, and behavior which may or may not conform to socially defined behaviors and characteristics typically associated with being either masculine or feminine.
>
> —CENTER FOR HEALTH AND LEARNING

Lastly, for some of us, neither "man" nor "woman" accurately encompasses how we identify.

> Nonbinary describes someone who does not identify within the gender binary. For some folks this means identifying somewhere between the binary "ends" (male and female), for some it means identifying as a combination of genders, and for others it means feeling a complete lack of a gender. For many folks, being nonbinary entails liberation from the stereotypes and gender roles attached to the gender they were assigned at birth.
>
> —SCHUYLER BAILAR

Finally, during the lockdown, I had found words that articulated exactly what I'd been feeling all through childhood and deep into my adulthood, a feeling I ended up burying as I thought I was the only one who was wrestling with it. Also, I think it's important to note that for me, a lot of privilege came with being a "boy" or a "man," so it wasn't like I was crying myself to sleep over this. I was too busy navigating the obstacles that came with my race and sexuality. If anything, my gender was the only thing that wasn't causing me any strife. (This isn't the case for every nonbinary person, but just my own experience.) The intersections of my gender with race and sexuality created personal friction. But with this new definition and going down a rabbit hole of watching and listening to other nonbinary folx speak of their experience, I felt seen in a way I hadn't felt before. I thought I had when I found friendships with other Black gay men, but this was different. This was fuller, more whole. This was being seen in the totality of my identity. I was overwhelmed by that and incredibly scared.

The tears that my dog licked off my face that afternoon were not from the relief but from the fear. I'd accepted my manhood and created a career and platform wanting to champion Black gay men. And suddenly I felt I was about to be an outsider yet again. During college, I'd started to reckon with intersectionality. I gained a community of Black and Latine friends, gay and straight. Some of my closest Black friends and I started having Black sleepovers in our senior year. We knew all too well what it was to be at a PWI, and our Black sleepovers were a time for us to commune, eat, drink, laugh, and talk about the real shit going on in our hearts.

Some of my favorite life memories are from those sleepovers, where we busted out into improv songs and danced about good dick or wiped each other's tears as we shared our fears and hopes for our futures. Even though most of the women in our sleepover group were straight, all the men (except one) were gay. So it was this space where my Black gay manhood was on full display and in full value. Shortly after graduating college, I got into a serious relationship with Kevin, a Latine man I lived with at the time my mother became a born-again Christian. Kevin and I were both interested in cultivating and spending time in Queer POC spaces, which allowed me to gain some deeper friendships, specifically with Queer Black and brown men.

In my thirties, after moving to LA, I was inspired by a friend, author Sasha Sagan, who founded the Ladies Dining Society—a monthly dinner where a curated list of women would meet, eat, drink, and commune—to begin a Brothers Dining Society. Mine was specifically for Black/Latine/POC Queer men, and, if I do say so myself, the joy at our dinners was unmatched.

I found a safety in all these spaces because of our shared experiences. I treasured that belonging, especially with the other Black gay men, and was terrified that now I'd have to give it up. After finally being in love with my identity and finally gaining success in Hollywood without having to be in the closet or act masc all the time, now I feared I had to uproot all of that. I was also afraid of disappointing other Black gay men or being perceived as "embarrassed" of being a Black gay man. Many Black gay men spend their childhoods fighting to prove their manhood, especially those who are fem. Then, at some point, many learn to take control of their narrative and identity and say, "I am Black, I am gay, and I am a man." There's an importance in taking the word "man" back. There's an importance in seeing Black gay men stand proudly in their manhood. Such representation matters. So the notion that I would suddenly say, "I'm not a man" made my stomach churn. Why give up this thing I fought so hard to redefine and reclaim?

This "man" thing is complex, though. For Queer folx and women, it's ingrained in us that emasculating a cisgender heterosexual man is one of the worst things you can do. We hear all the time on TV programs or in films or in the real world: "Make sure he feels like the man." "Make sure he knows he's the man." "Let him be the man." When you add Black to that "man," you can understand that the mandate not to emasculate a Black father, son, or brother is rooted in the way that white supremacy actively sought to do just that. When Black men were able to claim some of their power (and by the way, Black men are still trying to do just that but continue to be shot down, alongside Black women and folx), many borrowed the same tools of oppression used in the name of white supremacy and applied them to Black gay men, viewing Black gay men as an embarrassment and an attack on "the good Black man" just through the mere act of existing.

I can't speak to the cis-het male experience, but as a Queer person who identified as a man most of my life, the fight to reclaim that word can be an arduous one filled with resilience and very little healing. Some of us claim our manhood through building our bodies so that we're lean and muscular, while others reject anything feminine, even our fem peers. Some blatantly rebel against societal norms, reveling in our femininity and declaring that we're just as much of a man as the straight ones. That last option, I think, is the hardest to achieve yet the most ideal. Then again, if you never name the pain from the rejection—the anger—your rebellion stays rooted in proving something, as opposed to just living. That said, I think that last option is the most fitting, because, truly, what defines who gets to be a man? Let me say that again: What defines who gets to be a man? Some say that it's your genitalia or your heterosexuality, while others believe that it's your masculinity—how "butch" or "manly" you are.

I don't know what the definition of a "man" is or should be, but I do know it should include anyone who deems themselves one. An individual's gender identity shouldn't be based on outside affirmation. Others should affirm it because the individual has stated who and what their gender is. Our gender is *our* journey and *our* experience.

The reality is that fighting for a penis-having, straight-identifying, masculine person to be the only one who dons the word "man" has nothing to do with science, God, or anything remotely intellectual, but has everything to do with upholding patriarchal norms that allow a toxic demographic to hold on to power by oppressing others. And many oblige and subscribe to that oppression with sentiments like: *We can't emasculate the straight dude, so let's tell him his irrational and harmful behavior is completely justified.* When a gay, trans, or Queer person identifies as a man, some people believe that somehow diminishes, tarnishes, or devalues the experience of manhood. Spoiler alert: It doesn't. "Man" is not some exclusive club that loses its cool factor once too many people start attending. It's gender. There's not one correct, linear experience that validates somebody's gender identity.

With that in mind, and with my husband's unwavering support, I borrowed some of his confidence in me and decided to connect with a few nonbinary folx on social media. One of them connected me with a few of their friends, and I spent the day speaking to various folx about their experiences and taking in their supremely thoughtful advice. By the end of it all, I felt less scared, because the through line from each person was: "It's your experience and nobody else gets to define it."

There's sometimes pressure to be what the world thinks nonbinary is, which can mean androgynous or gender nonconforming.

Gender nonconforming: Denoting or relating to a person whose behavior or appearance does not conform to prevailing cultural and social expectations about what is appropriate to their gender.

—OXFORD DICTIONARY

I'm the first to admit that I'm far from androgynous, and I present very much as the societal expectations of "man," but it doesn't make me any less nonbinary. The folx I spoke to encouraged me to own my identity. Suddenly, the thing that I'd surrendered to believing didn't exist actually existed. Suddenly, the space in the world opened up, and I belonged to myself in a more complete way than I knew was possible.

But getting to that sense of belonging wasn't easy, and I'm still figuring it out. It wasn't like the seas parted and the birds started chirping and suddenly Michelle Obama's on my speed dial inviting me to her house for a kiki. Far from it. Yes, I felt a weight lifted off me, so I knew I was on the right track, but I wasn't ready to broadcast my identity to everyone until I really knew what it would mean for my life. I had many questions, like: What are my pronouns now? How am I supposed to act now? What changes and what stays the same now?

Daunting questions, and in some respects the wrong ones. Or maybe not the wrong ones (easy on the judgment), but not important ones, because I'm still me. Just like when I began identifying as gay, I'm still me, with the freedom to experience, explore, and build up pride along the way.

Even identifying as nonbinary, I still use he/him/his pronouns, but I've also added they/them/theirs to the mix. I like to say that my "he" pronouns are for the world, and my "they" pronouns are for me, my close loved ones, and anyone else who chooses to use them. This is because for me, my race and my sexuality still pose much more of a battle in my everyday life than my gender, so emotionally I don't have the bandwidth to correct people on my pronouns. One day I might, and I may choose to exclusively use "they" pronouns. Or I might decide to exclusively use "he" pronouns again. Neither decision makes me any more or less nonbinary, in the same way that knowing or not knowing the lyrics to a DMX song doesn't make me more or less Black, and watching or not watching *Drag Race* doesn't make me more or less gay. I'm me. Always me.

At this stage in my life, when people call me "a man," I don't usually correct them or push back. This shift in my gender identity is still new for me, and though I've made it public knowledge, it's a personal journey. Right now, I don't feel compelled to have long conversations about my gender identity, because it's still mine. It's still this thing that I'm discovering and peeling the layers back on and swimming in the nuances of. And the thing that I want to impress upon anyone navigating sexuality, gender, and life is that things are allowed to change. Fluidity is a beautiful thing.

The last thing that is important to me to say is if you see yourself in any part of me or my identities, I'm honored to be that reflection. I'm proud to represent Black folx, Black Queer folx, Black nonbinary folx, Black gay men, and all Black men. I'm proud to be represented by Black folx, Black Queer folx, Black nonbinary folx, Black gay men, and all Black men. I consider myself part of all those communities. And that's the real privilege.

You are not responsible for living out the fears or
expectations of others.
You have no responsibility to hold on to their
own truths and traumas.
You are your own.
—RACHEL CARGLE

BUILDING CONFIDENCE

If you're looking for some thoughts on building confidence, read this...

Don't force yourself to be understood by people committed to misunderstanding you.

You lose power when you let others define you. If you try to be who others say you SHOULD be, you'll always come up short. Don't let them put you in a box. You're too special to be caged.

Remove the people from your life who don't champion you, don't encourage you, and don't hold space for your dreams. Replace them with a community where mutual respect, love, and support are the standard.

Everyone can believe in you, but when YOU believe in yourself, that's when your power can be expressed fully.

Make self-love your strongest muscle.

Your confidence is worth mastering. Practice affirming yourself. Practice loving yourself. Commit to it, and eventually you'll accept nothing less.

You got this. You are enough. You belong. Your perspective is valuable. Your presence is necessary. And in case you haven't heard it yet today, you are deeply loved.

4. They

WENT TO DINNER RECENTLY WITH a new friend—Black, gay, curly hair, and a few years older than me, in his early forties. It was our first time having a one-on-one, and so our dinner was spent asking each other questions about family, career, experiences of the past, and hopes for the future. As we were just about to ask for the check, my new friend noticed I was wearing a gold name plate that spelled out *THEY*. He asked if "they" was my pronoun or if it stood for something else. I proceeded to give the spiel I usually give: "I'm nonbinary, and my pronouns are he/him/his and they/them/theirs. I like to say my 'they' pronouns are for me, and my 'he' pronouns are for everyone else, because I recognize that I present as a man."

"Yes, you are a Black man," he said. His tone was authoritative, like he thought I had forgotten myself and wanted to make sure that I knew I was, in fact, a *man*. I was taken aback, but I try to avoid confrontations, so I received what he said and didn't make a big deal out of it.

"Sure, yes, and I'm nonbinary," I said, and we left it at that.

Now before I dive deeper into this, I want to stress this person and I are new friends, and this exchange happened during our first time hanging out. At the time of me writing this, I don't know his stance on nonbinary folx, and I didn't ask, as I was managing my own insecurities in that moment.

I have this inner battle with holding both my identity and how I'm identified at the same time. How do I hold space for both experiences and represent both experiences, being nonbinary and a Black man? When my new friend said, "You are a Black man," a defiance grew in me. A *Don't tell me what I am!* type of feeling. And almost immediately after that, I thought, *What am I?* As in, am I what I say I am, or what others say I am?

Sure, in an ideal world, we're all what we say we are. That's the way it should be. But for the purposes of transparency, vulnerability, and deeper understanding, let's discuss what happens before one builds the confidence to own one's identity regardless of what others think.

For me, there's this out-of-body awareness of knowing that I identify in a way that people physically can't see while knowing that my experiences are based on what they physically *can* see. Both experiences—what people can and can't see, what they can and can't identify—make up who I am. Both experiences impact my internal and external lives. Both experiences leave me struggling to stand my ground in how I identify, because as much as I deserve to have how I identify respected, I also want to acknowledge what I'm experiencing.

Yes, you are a Black man.

I have an internet friend who I find comfort in following, and hopefully by the time this book comes out we'll have met IRL. David Lopez is a gorgeous nonbinary, Latine makeup artist and hairstylist who, like me, uses he/they pronouns. On their Instagram, they'll post photos in glamorous looks wearing gorgeous wigs with a perfectly beat face and lined-up beard. Then they'll post photos exposing their muscled body in "boy clothes." They're stunning in every iteration. I know they also deal with people questioning their gender identity and fluidity. In one of their posts, they're wearing a wide-brim hat with an unbuttoned, white long-sleeved shirt perfectly tucked into baby-blue slacks. They truly look as though they stepped off a Prada runway. In their caption, they write:

> Non-binary/gender fluid people don't owe you a presentation that looks androgynous to you. We don't owe you a presentation that looks like what you consider to be feminine or masculine.

I couldn't agree more, and yet there's this piece of me that nags: *Maybe I should present more fluid. More feminine.* Perhaps if I were to present more androgynously, people would assume I'm a "they" and maybe even accept my gender identity. But that plays right into the hands of doing what society wants instead of doing what I want.

When I was stepping into my nonbinary identity, I had a conversation with a nonbinary, gender-nonconforming person of South Asian descent who was giving me some guidance on how to navigate my reckoning. "You're going to have it harder because you're Black," they said to me plainly.

Oh goodie, I thought. I could faintly hear my mother saying, "Why would you choose to be gay? It's going to be harder." Obviously, this person wasn't saying that my nonbinary identity was a choice, but there was an acknowledgment that it could make things challenging in a different way. That I wouldn't be able to detangle it from my race. That it wouldn't be this thing I could reckon with in some artificial vacuum of gender.

Black manhood and masculinity are held in such high esteem in the community. I guess I assumed there would be pushback around my nonbinary identity from cis-het Black people because I had experienced that with my gayness and fem-ness. I suspected there could be pushback from gay Black men, especially from an older age group, because they'd fought so hard with straight Black people to be seen fully as men, to not have their gayness strip them of their manhood. They fought that fight for themselves, and for me.

So when my new friend said, "You are a Black man," I felt like I'd done something wrong. Like maybe I was wrong. Like sharing my "they" pronouns had disrespected the fights he fought. Or perhaps he thought he was being supportive in reminding me, "You are a Black man." In that moment, my confidence in my nonbinary identity wavered. I'm human, and even though being nonbinary may not be new to me, being aware of and identifying as such is. I don't have the same roots planted that I have in other areas of my identity, so it's understandable that someone challenging me could inspire internal pause. But ultimately, baby, I know who I am. And I'm proud to be who I am.

It wasn't that my new friend was wrong about me presenting as a Black man, having the experience of a Black man, living as a

Black man, or being a Black man. The issue was that his assertion was meant to deny my nonbinary identity. But after some time to reflect, the experience gave me more language and confidence to explain why I use both pronouns.

Yes, I've said publicly that at this point in my life, I have enough to deal with as it relates to me learning how to stand in my truth, love my identity, and speak up for my Black Queerness. I don't have the capacity to correct people on pronouns and inevitably hold space for their emotions when they fuck it up. I'm already reckoning with my own emotions.

So "they" is for me, and "he" is for everyone else. "They" is especially for little Brandon who didn't quite feel like a boy or a girl, who couldn't decide between playing Mr. Brandon or Miss Tana. "He" is also for little Brandon who promised not to be like his absent father, who promised to be a better man and a better father one day. "He/they" is for adult Brandon who wants to honor both experiences, who knows that how I identify and how I am identified equally shape the person I am. Who believes that not everything has to be this or that. Who's learning to trust the gray areas of life and multiple truths.

Instead of choosing to fit into a box, I choose to expand into my life.

"He/they" is my expansion.

Be proud of who you are,
not ashamed of how someone else sees you.
—UNKNOWN

BLACK AND QUEER AND FREE

In these times, I find it imperative to celebrate the beauty in my Black and the rebellion in my Queer, and to swim deeply in a space between masc and fem.

I release who I thought I could be.

I reject who I was told I should be.

And I dance in a dom(inance) of free.

I marvel at the simplicity of my complexities and bask in the complexities of my humanity.

I find peace outside of your expectations and peace inside of divine ordination.

I find peace in the burrow of my grandmother's dreams, and peace in the complexion of her eyes. Her eyes that saw me before I saw myself.

Her eyes that knew me long before there was anything to know.

I step into my life, using the pieces of her worldly sacrifices as my shelter, as my altar, as my wings. Letting her whispers guide me to an Eden of unconditional love for my Black, my Queer, and the deep expansive waters of my free.

5. YouOnSomeFuckShitVille

N THE SUMMER OF 2020, as the world, specifically America, was reckoning with racial justice, I made a video with my husband, Matthew, a gentlehearted white guy with the sweetest smile and very nice arms (ha ha) about being in an interracial marriage. It was an attempt to thoughtfully share how we as a couple were navigating what was happening in the world to me as a Black person up against white supremacy, and how we reconcile that inside of a relationship where I'm married to a white person.

A friend of mine told me he shared that video with a Black friend who's also in an interracial marriage with a white partner, and it wreaked havoc in their relationship. As I understand it, the way Matthew expressed how he shows up in the fight for racial justice and supporting me was not what this Black friend's white partner was doing. In fact, it sounded like the white partner wasn't doing a damn thing, and it was causing his husband to reevaluate their partnership.

Obviously, the intent of our video wasn't to create tension in other marriages, but I think the murder of George Floyd and the rise of Black Lives Matter forced a lot of us to reassess the white people we're in relationships with, be it romantically, professionally, or personally.

Comedian and actress Amanda Seales often says that there are "people who are white" and "people who happen to be white." The first describes people who are complicit in and perpetuate the harmful natures of whiteness and the privilege it carries. The latter describes people who are aware of their privilege but do everything in their power to dismantle it and create equity wherever they are. I can confidently say that when it comes to white friends, I only have relationships with white people committed to fighting for my life and the lives of Black folx everywhere. Anybody else gets a one-way ticket to YouOnSomeFuckShitVille, a place where you can be your toxic self without harming others. And I wish them... nothing.

But I'm sometimes shaken when I meet a Black person surrounded by white friends who clearly wear their privilege unapologetically. The types who "don't see race." I can't judge, though, because I definitely had a few of those friends in my life up until my early twenties. In my opinion, the way to sever those relationships and make sure you never find yourself in them again is to acknowledge that white supremacy is a very real thing. But before I personally became aware of the ways in which white supremacy was running rampant in the world, I first had to become aware of the ways in which it was running rampant in me. It was a relationship with a white classmate of mine that sparked my awakening.

But it wasn't just any relationship. He was my first love. I've already told you a little about him earlier—Pink Soap friend—but if you'll indulge me, I'd like to tell you our love story.

On the final night of my freshman year at NYU, I spent the evening with a few friends who were headed back to their hometowns for the summer. Being a native New Yorker, I would just be going back to Queens.

We met up at the Thai restaurant across the street from my dormitory—the same one I came out to Mycah in front of a year later—where the bartender, a white gay man, used to serve us nineteen-year-olds some strong-ass drinks. I can't remember everyone who was there, but for sure my friend Ruth (we're still friends today), her dormmate (who a few months later would become my Pink Soap friend), and his sister were in attendance.

Pinky (as I'll call him for short) was gorgeous—a six-foot-three white boy with brown hair, a lean body, gentle eyes, small-town charm, and a deep love for Lil' Kim. He fell into the "people who happen to be white" category. He was a social work major with an insatiable desire to make the world a more equitable place.

He was also straight.

I'd met Pinky a few times over our freshman year, but that night was my first time hanging out with him. I was still in the closet and repressing any sexual feeling toward men, so I can't say that I found myself lusting after him, but I still enjoyed his energy. He was quite funny, and the quickest way to my heart, romantically or platonically, is to make me laugh.

After a few whiskey sours, our chemistry started to grow. We were finishing each other's sentences, enjoying each other's jokes.

Then the group decided that we should go to our friend's penthouse around the corner. (Yes, honey, many of the kids at NYU had beaucoup-beaucoup dough.) So we paid our tab and stumbled up Fourteenth Street into an apartment building on the corner of Union Square. When we arrived at floor PH, our friend already had drinks waiting for us.

Being that there was so much space (as penthouses are known for), we all found our little pockets to socialize in. I sat on a white couch, which sat across from a second white couch, separated from each other by an expensive-looking glass coffee table. In my drunkenness, I decided I wanted to read one of the magazines on the table. After a moment, I looked up and saw Pinky sitting across from me. We didn't say anything, but he had a look in his eyes, focused on me. I certainly didn't think it was sexual, because he was such a "dude" and I'd convinced myself at the time that I was also a "dude," just with feminine tendencies. We held each other's gaze for about five seconds, and then I went back to reading while he joined his sister in the kitchen. I didn't think anything more of it.

The next day I received a text from him. More specifically a BBM—yes, honey, a BlackBerry Message. Before the iPhone, BlackBerrys were the must-have device for all us cool-ass kids. Pinky had gotten my number from Ruth and reached out just to chat. Or so he said, at first. Our in-person chemistry translated seamlessly over text. As the summer progressed, we chatted every day except for the two days he went camping and didn't have service. Sometime in mid-July, he asked for my home address. A few days later, I received a letter in the mail. A handwritten letter. It was the sweetest thing any friend had ever done for me, and so unexpected from a straight guy friend. It put the biggest grin on my face . . . and butterflies in my stomach.

The butterflies quickly brought concern. People don't get butterflies in their stomach over friends. And I'd read the letter ten times, my heart racing faster with each read. It was literally him writing stream-of-consciousness thoughts about his day at the office where he had a summer job. The content of the letter was cute, because he's funny, but him wanting to write to me was what made it special. I clearly had a crush but didn't dare say that out loud, because I didn't want to be gay, and I didn't want to ruin this friendship that I'd come to treasure so much.

Sophomore year, Pinky was slated to be an RA and I was to be a mentor for incoming freshmen in the drama department, which meant that both of us were returning to campus a week before school started. That week was full of parties, alcohol, and sex, but since I wasn't sleeping with either girls or boys, I was just there for the parties and booze.

Pinky and I had eagerly been waiting to see each other again, and he invited me to a little gathering happening in his dorm apartment. (NYU dorms—apart from a few of the freshmen ones—are actual New York City apartment buildings.)

I showed up in my purposely distressed jeans, a striped button-down, and a white visor cocked to the side. Yes, a muthafuckin' white visor. My fashion game wasn't quite as on point as my mother's yet. I was trying, but my God, was it off at times. Pinky met me downstairs to sign me in, and he looked . . . perfect. I swear there was a light orbing around him. The lump in my throat couldn't have been bigger. My stomach felt like I was being dropped out of the sky over and over and over again. We hugged, but only briefly, because I was trying to stay "manly" (in my white visor), and then I got a whiff of his cologne.

When we got upstairs, I went right for the alcohol to calm my nerves. The night was going, and it felt great to be back in the presence of Pinky and to meet some of his friends. But in my effort to keep playing it cool and not let on to Pinky (or his friends) that I had a deep, passionate crush on him, I drank a little too much. And because I'm not the type of gal who wants someone holding my hair back in the bathroom, I decided I was going to leave and go back to my dorm, which was downtown by South Street Seaport. At that late hour, it would have taken about forty minutes by subway to get there, so if I had a shot at making it and not passing out on the train in the process, I needed to leave immediately. As I was gathering my stuff, Pinky, also drunk, intercepted me.

"Are you leaving?" he said.

"Yeah, I'm tired, and I should head out," I replied.

"Well, my roommate isn't here for another few days, so you can crash in his bed...if you want."

And I most definitely wanted to, partly for the opportunity to spend more time with Pinky, but also because at this point, a bed six feet away felt far more appealing than a bed that was a ride on the 6 train away. I happily took him up on his offer.

Pinky led me to his room, where I lay down on his roommate's bed while he rested on his a few feet away. Both of us were drunk but still lucid and coherent. The room was dark, with just one beam from the moon piercing through the window. Pinky lay on his back, and I turned over on my side, facing the wall. We were quiet. Then he said, "I want something." Then there was a pause. I waited for him to say more, but he didn't, so I replied:

"What do you want?"

"I want Brandon."

It felt like a trap. I wanted Pinky so badly, but I didn't believe there was a world in which this beautiful (straight) giant wanted me. "I want you too," I longed to say, but I feared the minute those words left my mouth, our room would be stormed by some of the other partygoers yelling, "Told you he was a faggot!"

I couldn't risk being humiliated or bullied. I didn't want to give anyone ammunition to hurt me, so I laughed, facing the wall, and said, "Prove it." I thought if this was a trick to out me, I could laugh it off and maintain my straightness. But if it wasn't a joke, and he really did want me, this was his chance to have me.

A few seconds later, I heard the creak of his double mattress frame. I heard his footsteps as he went from his side of the room to mine. I looked over my shoulder, and there he was, standing over me. He climbed into my bed, I got a waft of that cologne again, and my heart started to race once more. *This isn't happening. This is a joke,* I thought.

Then he kissed me.

It was the most perfect kiss. A kiss that made me feel safe, desired, and yes, valued. He wanted me. I wanted him. And that night we both got what we wanted ... until, of course, the pink soap started to burn my hole! But once it cooled off—I can't believe I'm writing about my hole cooling off—we did other things, and it was beautiful.

At this point in my young life, I had hooked up with a fair number of girls, but this was different. It was more than just the obvious difference of sleeping with a man. This felt like every great love story ever told.

I would always hear my straight classmates and friends talk about their relationships, talk about being in love and marriage and partnership. Sure, I had girlfriends in the past to whom I said "I love you," but that night with Pinky made me realize I'd never actually been in love. He was also the first person ever that I could see myself having a family with, which seemed monumental to me at the time. I came from a single-parent household, so I never imagined co-parenting being part of my life, and especially not co-parenting with another man. But Pinky was special.

Yes, now I'd obviously be like, "Girl! You barely know this man. How you already planning to raise kids with him?!" But I was nineteen and I felt like I knew him. Even before that night, we'd talked so much over the summer, and those butterflies began to feel like love. Again, I was nineteen and exploring my sexuality much later than a lot of my peers, so it was easy to have love, lust, sex, and fantasies of marriage and parenting entangled with one another.

Even still, with all the emotion rushing through my veins, the reality was that both of us were still very closeted. So, as I mentioned before, instead of fucking in our dorm rooms, we spent the next few months fucking in bathrooms, stairwells, and empty offices. If we saw each other in public, we presented as friends. Acquaintances, even. We numbed ourselves to pull that off. It was painful. It was also kind of hot. I would see boys looking at him when we walked down the street, and I never got jealous because I knew he only wanted me.

But as they say, all good things come to an end.

After winter break, Pinky was slated to study abroad in Ghana. The plan was for him to go home for the holidays and then fly to Ghana after Christmas, meaning I wouldn't see him until fall of our junior year. Nine months. But it shouldn't have mattered, because we weren't boyfriends. We weren't in a relationship. Hell, we weren't gay. So why was I so upset?

I wanted him to go. He was so excited about the trip. I wanted that for him. But I couldn't understand what I was feeling. I can now tell you it was heartbreak and the dread of missing him, but I hadn't a clue about how to handle the emotions swirling around in my heart.

The reality is, Pinky was my first boyfriend, even though we never called each other that.

Before he went home for winter break, we had one more night together. All my roommates had already left town, so I had the apartment to myself. Pinky came over for the very first time, and we watched *The Lion King* while we made love. (Hold your judgment, babe!) It wasn't like our stairwell or bathroom sex. This was comfortable and intimate and tender and meaningful.

Afterward, as I lay with his long arms wrapped around me, inhaling his sweet cologne, he asked me for the first time, "Do you have feelings for me?" Almost four months since we started hooking up, and *now* he wanted to know? But just like our first night, I thought this might be a prank. That perhaps my roommates hadn't actually gone home, and if I said that I did have feelings, they'd suddenly burst through the door and cackle at my admission. And most importantly, saying yes would mean I was, in fact, gay. Fucking a guy, I could write off as two friends "exploring." Having feelings for a guy, well, that's just ... gay.

"No," I said. "Do you have feelings for me?"

"No," he replied.

We cuddled for another hour or so before he left, and he promised to see me next fall.

A month into his semester in Ghana, I met another guy. Smith, the tall white dude who was okay with me not being out yet. Then, one afternoon, Pinky called me from Ghana.

"I have to tell you something," he said.

"What's up?"

"I love you," he said.

My heart stopped. Someone loved me. A man loved me. Pinky, the man who put butterflies in my stomach and made me feel like I was being dropped out of the sky over and over and over, loved me.

"I love you, too," I said.

I could hear his joy. I could feel it. It was the same as mine. And even though I was dating this other guy, I meant what I said. I had wanted to say it to him since I received that handwritten letter.

We hung up the phone, both excited to be loved, and then...

This is the reason I think it's so imperative to learn how to love yourself. If you don't know how to love yourself, you can't accept love from others. You'll always think there's a catch. Always think a prank is being played on you. And I did.

When I hung up with Pinky, I was literally floating. But only for ten minutes. After ten minutes, I thought, *He's lying. He can't love me. And if he does, he won't see me for months. He won't be in love with me in the fall.*

This spiral sank its teeth into me and wouldn't let go. The next day, against the will of my heart, I called Pinky back and said, "I don't love you."

He was quiet. I could hear his shock. I could feel his confusion. His disbelief that this was happening. "What do you mean?!" he asked. I repeated myself. I could feel him revert into social worker mode. Eerily calm. Respectful. Understanding. He took a breath and then said, "Okay. I have to go." He hung up.

I'm not sure if I believe in regrets, because everything that's happened has created who I am today, but if I did have one regret in my life, it's that phone call. Not because maybe Pinky and I would have lived some fairytale ending; chances are very high that we would have broken up because of a myriad of reasons. But I regret allowing *my* trauma to traumatize him. I didn't believe I was worthy of love—that was my trauma—and so I took my love back from him. I hurt him before he could hurt me. No matter how you slice it, I deeply hurt someone I loved. And that, I regret.

That fall, we both came out of the closet independently of one another. We tried to get back together, but he didn't trust me. Understandably so. He had bared his heart to me. I told him I loved him too, and not even twenty-four hours later, I took it back.

We were on and off. One minute he wanted me, the next minute he didn't. I eagerly waited for him to call, over and over and over. And whenever he did, I dropped everything to be with him. And then he would ghost me, punishing me. But I held on to hope, because he was the first and only man I saw a future with. I didn't want anyone else. I also didn't think anyone else would ever want me, so the stakes of getting him back were high.

But by the middle of our junior year, a full year after I took back my love, we were finally over. He'd met someone.

I remember walking down Broadway and Eighth Street, openly weeping. I happened to be spotted by my friend Mackenzie, an effortlessly gorgeous white woman with curly brown hair and a soothing voice, on her way to class.

"B!" she hollered.

I peered up, and I guess I looked like a mess because her face turned into deep concern. Without me saying anything, she asked, "Pinky?"

I nodded and replied, "It's over." And then I fell into her arms.

It was my first breakup, even though we were never in what we would have called a relationship.

I didn't eat. I didn't sleep. I just cried and cried and cried some more. After two months, I had no more tears. Instead, I became a shell of a person. Unable to function. I lost my sense of purpose and lost the will to do or be anything. I can't remember if someone suggested it or if I came to the decision myself, but at the three-month anniversary of our breakup, I decided to go to counseling.

My family considered therapy "white-people shit." It wasn't something that they supported or believed in. To them, Jesus was capable of handling all our troubles. But Jesus was taking his sweet-ass time helping me through this breakup, so I signed up for a session with one of the NYU therapists.

She was a petite woman with long reddish hair and a neutral disposition. Not cold, not warm either. Just neutral. We spent the hour talking about Pinky and my fears of being alone and not being lovable. "But you're a charming and attractive young man," she said. "What makes you think you'll never find love again?"

"No matter how attractive someone might think I am, I'll never be as attractive as a white man," I replied.

I didn't think I'd said anything crazy until I saw the horror on this woman's face. She truly could have handed me a ticket to YouOnSomeFuckShitVille! For the first time, I recognized that my trauma was deeper than just being lovable, deeper than just feeling worthy of love. Was deeper than a breakup. Neither I nor the NYU therapist had the words for it, but let's just say white supremacy had entered the chat.

Though it would take years before I could connect the ways in which white supremacy had worked on me, my relationship to Pinky was my awakening. That said, my relationship to Pinky was also sacred and beautiful. Two things get to be true. I was deeply in love with a very special boy, and I was deeply in love with my proximity to his white privilege. A gray space.

The shadow side of my relationship to him was that I felt on top of the world when I dated him because I thought it validated me. I thought it protected me. I thought it made *me* belong.

Human nature is to desire love, to desire being seen and accepted. Pinky's whiteness did all of that for me, or so I thought. But I hadn't realized that I had those sentiments until my exchange with the NYU therapist.

My Blackness and gayness had been positioned as obstacles in my life. They were things I couldn't change, but I could get as close to acceptance as possible by dating a tall, white Prince Charming. Or so I thought. But this was a shortcut and an avoidance of the dark underbelly of self-hatred that had been brewing, dictating my every move.

For twenty years, I'd absorbed the fact that Black people were disproportionately underestimated, locked up, shot down, and discarded in America. Gay people were beat up, bullied, and discarded as well. I didn't want that to happen to me, so white men became my shield of protection. My way of being gay but a "respectable gay." A "respectable Black gay." I could throw up at how deep in the Sunken Place I was. But as it turns out, dating white men only fed my self-hatred, because I'd yet to find self-love. Dating white men only highlighted that I still thought something was wrong with me.

For the next year and a half after Pinky, I went on dates and hooked up with a lot of white dudes in mostly drunken one-night stands. Some I even dated, but nothing longer than two or three months. With each guy I hooked up with, I found myself thinking of Pinky. Wishing they were him. Wishing they smelled like him. Wishing that their kisses felt like his. That their bodies felt like his. As time went on, I gave up on finding someone like Pinky, but still, the guys were around six foot two, masculine, and white. I missed being "respectable" so much that I was allowing myself to be fetishized and tokenized by some trash-ass white men, all in the name of acceptance and safety.

It would take five years after that session with the NYU therapist, a bevy of too many flings, one serious boyfriend (who was Latine), and a fracture in my relationship to my now born-again Christian mother before I would really begin to do some intentional work on myself, to heal the collateral damage done from being raised in a white supremacist country.

I've mentioned that my husband, Matthew, is white, which understandably might bring up questions about being with him for proximity to privilege. The difference is I became aware of that trap before Matthew and I met. I did my self-work, and once I had an understanding of my toxic behaviors, I made a shift. I began to see my worth, which meant now when I dated a guy, I didn't look for him to be my missing half or a way for me to make myself respectable in the eyes of white people in power. Nothing was missing. And I was respectable because I was a caring and honest individual. Period. A man could add something different to my life, but they couldn't fill a space, because once I really started to love myself, there was no longer a space that needed filling. (Insert dick joke here.)

My husband can tell you that he put in work to be with me, because I was loud about my boundaries and I was never short on tickets to YouOnSomeFuckShitVille. I didn't need him to validate or affirm the beauty of my existence. I didn't need protecting, saving, or his privilege. So we built a relationship founded on our humanity.

Race *is* part of our relationship. It would be destructive, delusional, and dangerous if we weren't aware of our racial differences and his white privilege. And I believe there are some Black folx in relationships with white folx who "don't see race." I do believe there are Black folx who don't want to be seen as Black, who are consciously or unconsciously ashamed of their Blackness. The "color blindness" that both partners operate from allows the Black person to stay close to white privilege—or think they're staying close to it—while allowing the white person to ignore the ways in which they're complicit with a white supremacist society. They're always able to say "but my partner is Black" as a get-out-of-antiracism-work card. Worse, in gay relationships, many white partners use their sexuality as a reason why they don't have to do antiracism work. They assume that because they're gay, they understand *all* oppression.

They don't.

Black gay oppression is not white gay oppression. To be rejected by society because of your Blackness, then rejected again because of your sexuality, and then rejected again because of their intersections (we haven't even touched gender)—that's a different battle from what a white gay person endures. That's spending your life on the outside of *every* room and *every* system, and human nature makes you want to desperately crawl your way back into the good graces of (white) society, to change yourself or deny pieces of yourself so that you might be more palatable to (white) societal norms and standards. And if you're a Black person with a white partner who thinks your lived oppressions are the same, I'm telling you now with love and respect to wake the fuck up. A white person who can't acknowledge the ways in which Blackness is brutalized and Black Queerness is marginalized, especially inside the LGBTQIA+ community, cannot successfully support that Black person, because they don't think there's anything to support. They've convinced themselves that both of you move through the world with the same level of equality and equity. And as a Black person, if you aren't doing your own work, if you aren't committing to learn how to love yourself fully and you're still relying on others (specifically white others) to make you feel loved, you'll accept that bad behavior. You might even think you deserve it. You might even believe it's normal. It's not.

It's uncomfortable to name these truths, but I promise you I'm speaking from experience. I can say it because I've lived it. I ain't here to judge nobody, but if I can nudge someone awake, if I can help someone avoid years, decades even, of discarding themselves by bending to the whims of whiteness, then I'ma speak these truths.

As for my healing work, like I said, it didn't happen immediately. I would have to walk through a few more tribulations before I finally learned how to begin loving myself, and that love began with learning how to create boundaries.

The last place the colonizer leaves is your mind.

—HARI KONDABOLU

ABOUT MY (WHITE) HUSBAND

I love my husband. More than anything. More than anyone. (Except maybe our dog.) No partner has ever seen me more fully. No partner has ever wanted to expand with me more fully. No partner has ever loved me more fully.

I don't love "whiteness." I've found "whiteness" to be the most violent weapon and most insatiable threat to my life.

My husband is white. I don't love "whiteness." But I love my husband. And my husband is white.

My brain is always in chaos as I reckon with the psychology of whiteness, but periodically the reckoning intensifies when I am confronted with "whiteness" and my husband and their proximity to one another.

*　　*　　*

My husband also doesn't love "whiteness." He knows the violent weapon and the insatiable threat that it is. He knows the destruction it has caused and will continue to cause on my life and the lives of others if it's not dismantled. So, every day, I watch him dismantle his own whiteness. Dismantle his family's whiteness. Watch him rearrange his privilege to clear a path for Black equity. I watch him wrestle with who he was, who he is, who he wants to be. Who he wants to be for me. For our children. For our society.

I don't love "whiteness," but I love my husband.

$6.$ Author's Note: Holding Space

So I know we're only a few chapters in, and this is not the traditional place for an author's note, but I'm going to start talking about some really difficult shit for me. Family. I'm sure many of you can relate to how challenging families can be. The gray area is strong in this topic, and I feel the need to preface some things before we proceed.

A little behind-the-scenes for you: I'm writing this note during my "rewrite" phase of the book. A few months ago, I turned in the first draft of the complete manuscript, and now I'm going through the notes from my editors to clarify certain areas, polish others, and expound at will.

I received the notes about four weeks ago, had a meeting about them with my developmental editor, and was set to get to work on the second pass, which, as I'm typing, is due in a week. Every time I attempt to work on it, though, I freeze, or I distract myself with TV, social media, YouTube, or meetings. Yes, I'd rather be in a meeting than write. That's when you know there's some deeper shit happening.

Finally, I decided to talk to my therapist about the particular block I was having. It's not a creative one. All the words were there, chapters in place, and my editor has given me clear directions about what he's looking for in the updates. And still, it feels like there's a force field between me and my computer. Between me and this book.

My therapist reminded me that I had a similar force field when I was first writing but acknowledged this might be different because my body knows that this journey has required me to unearth a lot of moments that were never healed. Moments from my past that I experienced but never put into words. And this is the first time I'm doing that. It's a reckoning.

When I reckon, I have a tendency to go right for resilience, that word I'm so ambivalent about. I think a lot of Black folx and Queer folx—and especially Black Queer folx—have that tendency. We get hurt by someone or something, and we brush it off and keep forging ahead. We bounce back. We're strong. We're resilient. But as a result, I haven't named my pain. I've experienced things and perpetually said, "It's fine." I've made excuses for bad behavior. I've made excuses for betrayal and abandonment and racism and homophobia. I've given an abundance of grace in order to forgive and forget and be resilient.

As I told you earlier, my therapist always encourages me to name my actual feelings. I'd tell her something and follow it up with, "But it's okay."

And then she'd go: "No, it's heartbreaking." "It's tragic." "It's sad." She'd push me to name the feelings, because you can't heal the wounds you won't acknowledge. And you certainly can't heal them if you won't acknowledge how they truly feel. If "it's okay," then sure, you can get to resilience. You can move forward with your resilient Band-Aid, but eventually you'll bleed all over yourself.

In fairness, the coping mechanism of resilience has gotten me to this moment. I'm a thirty-four-year-old, Black, Queer, non-binary actor, writer, and activist, and by the time this gets into your hands, a published author. I have, in many regards, beat the system set up against someone like me. I've beat the odds and statistics, and that's been anything but easy. In fact, it's been painful, arduous, and exhausting. But I've never said that until right now. I always presented resilience. Always presented "it's fine." But resilience is not helping me get through writing this book. This book is challenging my sense of self. It's challenging what I thought I knew about myself.

I can feel myself bleeding.

If I have any hope of continuing to talk about these moments in my life, then I have to name my true feelings. I have to name the pain so that I don't just expose the wounds for your consumption and then slap some resilience on it. I can't put this book into the world and not have found healing in what I've shared. Doesn't need to be complete, as I do believe healing is a process. But I need to be on the path.

So...family. I love my family with every molecule that makes up my existence. I'm also angry at them, heartbroken by them. I wish that they'd protected me more. They protected my Blackness, but not my Queerness. And because those two things aren't separate—I'm not Black or Queer, I'm Black AND Queer—not protecting my Queerness means you're not protecting me.

I wish they saw value in my Queerness. I wish they held it sacred. They didn't, and so again, I'm angry and heartbroken. And

I'm scared to write that and put that in the world, because culturally, you don't talk about family business in public. But the resilience that I had to have in the face of not being protected, in the face of spending every single day scared, deep into my late twenties, won't take me further. I have to name the thing, and I hope in naming the pain, I might inspire someone reading this to name theirs. I hope they'll know you can love your family and still be heartbroken by them.

Full transparency: I'm itching to make excuses right now. Itching to put my pain aside and say something like "They did the best they could." And they did, and there'll be time for me to say that. But for a moment, I'd like for you to hold space with me in my anger and my heartbreak.

One of the most generous things you can do for another human is hold space for their feelings and their experience of something, especially a traumatic something.

When I'm the one holding space, I like to create an opportunity for someone to express their true feelings by asking, "How's your heart?" To me, there's a huge difference between "How are you?" and "How's your heart?" "How are you?" usually garners the stock answer "I'm fine." In my experience, "How's your heart?" instead invites a person to spill the real tea, to share what's going on internally—good, bad, or gray—and know that with me there won't be judgment. They won't have to feign happiness, make excuses, or apologize for their true feelings. They can experience freedom.

Holding space also means staying present and allowing a person to express what they're experiencing, whether it's about their relationship with you or something completely separate, without trying to change their experience, fix it, or give solutions. Solutions may be helpful later on, but in the moment of holding space, your only job is to listen to the other person without judgment. Chances are the person is already doing a lot of self-judgment on their own, so you serving as a safe, loving, and judgment-free resource is invaluable.

Sometimes the other person may be experiencing something that they haven't fully processed yet and aren't able to verbalize or articulate. Holding space might look like sitting in silence with them. It might look like physically embracing them—with their permission, of course. It might just be you reminding them that you love them and you're there for them.

Admittedly holding space can sometimes be challenging, so before you do so, make sure that you check in with *your* heart first. See if you have the emotional capacity to create that safe, loving, judgment-free space. It's totally okay if you can't sometimes, but just be honest with yourself about those moments so that when you do offer to hold space, you can show up fully for the other person.

Breathing as the person shares is one of the ways I stay present. As I breathe, I allow their story to come into my heart space, and I gently hold it there for them, using empathy to honor both their experience and their vulnerability in sharing said experience.

So, before I even begin to spill my own tea, I'm inviting you to hold space for and with me by taking three breaths, breathing in for a count of five and breathing out for a count of five.

Inhale

Exhale

Inhale

Exhale

Inhale
Exhale

From the depths of my heart, I thank you.

Worthiness doesn't have prerequisites.

—BRENÉ BROWN

---

7. Gay Stuff

MY HUSBAND, AN EDUCATOR, LIFE COACH, and soon-to-be therapist raised *outside* of New York City in Poughkeepsie, argues with me constantly about what time brunch should begin. He insists brunch takes place between nine a.m. and noon. I, a New York City native, couldn't disagree more. Now, sure, technically brunch is the words *breakfast* and *lunch* combined, symbolizing that it's a meal that exists in the space of those designated times. But any self-respecting brunch-goer knows that true brunch happens after twelve thirty p.m. Honestly, in my twenties, I'd say, "Don't send me a brunch invite that starts before one p.m. unless you hate me."

The order of events goes: Saturday night pregame, into dinner, into clubbing, into late-night eats at the local diner, into bed by four a.m. Sunday, wake up at eleven a.m. gasping for water, sit down in the shower while you chug a Gatorade, put on a pair of dark shades, hail a cab, and arrive at your one p.m. brunch around one thirty.

Am I lying? Where's the lie?

And then we brunch for hours, until the lights dim, candles get placed on the table, and your waiter says, "We're about to switch to our dinner menu. Is there anything else I can get you?" I'm proud to say there've been times where my party has said, "Yes, you can get us that dinner menu." That's how you brunch properly. I have plenty of friends who agree with this philosophy, including Kendyl.

About a year or so before I moved to LA, around the age of twenty-seven, I was in a cab with Kendyl, a woman around my age with a Southern accent paired with a New York City brashness—which I loved. The first time we met, we clicked instantly, because both of us love to eat, drink, and laugh. We had a few mutual friends, so often we only hung out in those groups. But one day, we finally decided we would get brunch together. She proposed a spot in Midtown where we could meet at around one-thirty-ish. (See? She knows!) After a few hours of guzzling mimosas and scarfing down anything on the menu that was fried, we decided to head to another restaurant in the Meatpacking District where one of those mutual friends was the manager—free drinks and dis-counted food, baby! We spent the fifteen-minute cab ride cackling about boys and work, and then we got on the topic of family. At this point, Kendyl knew I was thinking of moving to LA, and she said something like, "I bet your mom is going to miss you."

"Oh, I don't talk to my mother anymore," I responded without missing a beat. It fell out of my mouth casually, partly because of the mimosas and partly because it was common knowledge among my friends that I'd been estranged from my mother since I was twenty-four. Even though Kendyl and I had known each other for a few years, we were just starting to hang out one-on-one, so she wasn't privy to that information and her bubbly face fizzed out, becoming concerned.

Saying you don't talk to your mother always makes people pause, sometimes even eliciting judgment, as most people can't understand any reason you wouldn't have a relationship with a parent who's alive, not to mention living right over the bridge. I quickly explained. "My mother became a born-again Christian, and for me, being born the first time was enough," I said.

That was usually the joke I would tell whenever the bummer conversation of my parental relationship came up. It worked, and Kendyl laughed. She respectfully had no follow-up questions. I could see she didn't want to pry, but the conversation felt unfinished. We'd just spent hours bonding and sharing, and it felt important for me to give her a little more context without a joke or deflection. So I explained that my mother had taken issue with my sexuality and after a while I had to stop talking to her in order to protect myself.

Kendyl's face of concern turned into a deep understanding. "But you're so...so comfortable in your sexuality," she said. "So comfortable with who you are. I would have thought you were raised with a lot of acceptance. A house of rainbow flags." In Kendyl's defense, I was confidently wearing my Sunday brunch outfit of short shorts, a floral top, dark shades, and a wide-brim hat, so I could see why she'd think that I was brought up in a gay utopia.

Honestly, it was bittersweet to hear her assumption. On one hand, I was really grateful that I finally came off as someone who was comfortable in their skin, especially after so many years of being in denial about my sexuality. I mean, I was working very hard to love myself, to love being Black and Queer. But it was also sad to have to acknowledge that the love I'd found for my Queerness wasn't okay with my mother.

I came out to my mother when I was twenty years old in the detergent-and-cleanser aisle of the Whole Foods on Houston Street in downtown Manhattan. Not an exaggeration. At this point, all my friends knew I was gay, and I'd even begun dating a classmate very publicly. But I'd yet to tell my mother, and it felt "deceptive" (for lack of a better word). Historically, I told my mother everything. As an only child and a single parent, we were also best friends, and I was riddled with guilt for not having shared this part of myself. So, as she stood in front of an assortment of cleaning products, I quietly blurted out, "Mom, I'm bisexual."

When I first came out to Mycah and friends, I had said I was bisexual, but at this point I knew I was gay. But I think my young rationale was that I could perhaps ease the blow of my gayness by giving my mother a bit of hope that maybe I still could be with a woman. It didn't work. My mother just kind of stared at the detergent, not saying anything.

We're Caribbean, and my grandmother was a minister, so both my mother and I had very religious upbringings as PKs (pastor's kids). There's a different level of scrutiny, judgment, and expectation to live up to when you have a parent or grandparent who runs a church. You become the face of excellence and obedience and living "God's will." You have to attend prayer meetings and Sunday school, arriving to church early and leaving late. You're the poster child of God-fearing, God-loving kids. I like to say it's like being the local Sasha and Malia Obama. I believe that in many ways that pressure is what led my mother to leave the church when I was younger. She never left it completely, but she stopped attending services regularly in favor of searching for something that filled her cup more.

There were years when we subscribed to what's known as metaphysical teachings, which is basically a nondenominational, more spiritual approach to Christianity. I liked it because I could wear jeans to the church and services were an hour maximum, a far cry from the two- to three-hour services wearing a boxy suit I'd become accustomed to. There were also the days spent in Lifespring and Landmark, which were akin to life-coaching or personal-development courses. Some people refer to them as cults, while others say they've had transformative life experiences. Then there were the "Egyptian Priestess" days. I felt wildly uncomfortable there, because everything was steeped in a heterosexual male-female gender binary. And then came Buddhism. I felt safest there, but I also didn't have the willpower to chant and meditate for hours like my mother. I did love the chanting beads, though, because they were gorgeous. Other spiritual explorations followed.

By the time I came out to my mother in front of the laundry products, I was a junior at NYU and not attending any kind of religious institution. When my mom and I got back in the car, she finally found her words. "It's probably a phase," she said with a timbre of hope.

"It's not," I replied. "I can't change my sexuality, the way I can't change my Blackness."

She didn't respond. Her eyes stayed fixed on the road, and eventually we began a new topic of discussion. I never felt the need to speak about it again, but I was relieved that she knew.

By the time I turned twenty-three, I was a little over a year into my relationship with Kevin, the Puerto Rican–Ecuadorian man I mentioned earlier. Ironically, he and my mother had their own very sweet relationship. Kevin and I lived together in a Midtown apartment.

At the same time I was living with Kevin, my grandmother was nearing the end of her life.

My grandmother was very much my mother as well. She had the same level of authority (if not more) and influence (if not more). She was a force, an immigrant from Trinidad and the first person in our family to come to America. She worked as a nurse before becoming an ordained minister. As a Black woman minister, she broke many barriers and received awards for her work, including an honorary doctorate of ministry. But most importantly, she had an impact on more lives than I ever imagined.

As my grandmother's health was worsening, my mother started going back to church again. Reckoning with death has a way of luring people to anything that can contextualize the pain of loss.

Right before Thanksgiving, my grandmother took her last breath.

Hundreds upon hundreds of people showed up to her funeral to pay their respects to this icon that up until then I mostly knew as Grandma.

As you can imagine, her death was a devastating blow, and I was consumed in mourning, which completely blinded me to the forthcoming implosion. My mother had decided that she needed to rededicate her life to Jesus. So she became a born-again Christian. She was incredibly passionate about it, and I was happy that she'd found something that brought her peace in the midst of the greatest pain she'd ever faced.

One afternoon, while Kevin was out of town, my mother and I made plans for her to come over to the apartment for tea. I was so excited to show her how we'd decorated and really made the place feel like ours. I cleaned, picked up some bougie teas my mom loved, and laid it all out with side snacks. My mother arrived, and before I could even put the kettle on, she sat me down at the kitchen counter and asked me to read some passages from the Bible she'd brought with her. This wasn't cause for concern, because growing up with a minister for a grandmother meant reading the Bible was a mandatory activity in our house.

With her very stylish reading glasses on, my mother flipped to 1 Corinthians 6:9–10, which was already highlighted, and asked me to read aloud:

> Do not be deceived: neither the sexually immoral, nor idolaters, nor adulterers, nor men who practice homosexuality, nor thieves, nor the greedy, nor drunkards, nor revilers, nor swindlers will inherit the kingdom of God.

Sometimes, in the midst of a traumatic situation, your brain creates a new narrative because it refuses to accept the reality of what's happening. In this moment, I genuinely didn't associate myself with the passage, and there was no world in which I thought my mother was trying to tell me that it reflected her own beliefs. She was an actress, well known in the theater community, and many of my godparents and her best friends were gay. Plus she loved Kevin.

So at the end of reading the passage, I was truly confused and was about to ask a question, when she flipped to a second passage, Leviticus 20:13, and told me to read aloud:

> *If a man lies with a male as with a woman, both of them have*
> *committed an abomination; they shall surely be put to death;*
> *their blood is upon them.*

I knew that many Christians were homophobic and used the Bible to justify their bigotry, but neither my mother nor my grandma ever talked about homosexuality. So there had to be some other point she was trying to make.

Again, I was about to ask, when she flipped to a third passage, 1 Timothy 1:9–10, and told me to read aloud:

> *The law is not laid down for the just but for the lawless and dis-*
> *obedient, for the ungodly and sinners, for the unholy and profane,*
> *for those who strike their fathers and mothers, for murderers, the*
> *sexually immoral, men who practice homosexuality…*

I stopped reading and looked at her.

"Mom," I said. "What is this?"

"I just wanted you to know," she replied.

My mother was in the home that I shared with my boyfriend, making me read scriptures that declared my life a sin because she "just wanted me to know." I was baffled by the whole situation, and then suddenly she declared she had to leave. She'd been in my apartment all of ten minutes, just enough time to dismantle *everything* that I knew about myself and our relationship.

Gutted, I walked her to the door. "But I have gay godparents," I said. "You have gay friends. Are you saying this to them? Do you think their life is a sin?"

"They're not my son," she responded. My mother leaned in and kissed me on the cheek, then left, the perpetrator of a born-again Christian drive-by.

After that day, we would make dates to hang a few more times, but at each outing she would bring up how she was praying for me to marry a woman and how she hoped I would choose a different path. A different lifestyle. I would remind her that my sexuality wasn't a choice and asked that we "agree to disagree." She would seem to be okay with the request, but a few moments later, she would start spitting out the same rhetoric yet again.

Then she wanted to do weekly prayer calls. I love praying. To this day, I pray and meditate every morning. Back then, and in spite of everything that had transpired, a chance to pray with my mother, especially in the wake of my grandmother's death, sounded comforting. We would get on the phone and I'd pray for our health, safety, and success. Then she'd pray, also uttering prayers for my health, safety, and success, before seamlessly transitioning into a diatribe about saving my soul from the sins of homosexuality and finding me a wife. I would politely ask again for us not to talk about "gay stuff."

I was willing to have a relationship with my mother in which we didn't talk about dating, relationships, or anything remotely gay. I was willing to leave this piece of myself at the door for our relationship. "Just...let's not talk about it," I'd say over and over and over again. And over and over and over, she'd ignore that plea, citing her "motherly duty to save my soul."

Boundaries. I feel like toward the end of 2020, after almost a year of being in the pandemic, people started talking about "boundaries" more. It felt like a new topic for many. There was a palpable cultural conversation about needing to have them, wanting to learn how to create them. I suspect it's because everything happening from and within our homes was blurring lines for people about when to begin or end work and take space from someone you're living with.

Boundaries weren't exactly a new thing for me, because when I was a child, my mother taught me to respect the emotional boundaries of others. But I later came to realize she never taught me how to have my own. If she had, then one day I could apply boundaries to our relationship, and I don't think she ever wanted to give up ownership over me. And I do mean "ownership." It's very customary in Caribbean culture that a child continues to maintain the position of "child" deep into their adulthood. That means you're always obedient to any and every request from your parent, and if you dare to question their authority, heaven help you.

I'd like to believe that maybe it wasn't that she never wanted to release ownership, but rather she didn't know she was supposed to. But perhaps that's my trauma brain creating a palatable narrative, trying to be resilient. Even so, I still believe my mother's favorite saying: "Everybody is doing the best they can with what they know and have." Unfortunately, sometimes people's best can still be the most harmful.

All that said, my mother did teach me that if someone doesn't like you, doesn't like something about you, doesn't consider you, or disrespects you, then you gotta kick them to the curb. "You don't need that energy in your life," she would say. I think she was preparing me for how some people would treat me as a Black man, but I don't think she ever considered what would happen if I were gay. What would happen to *us* if I were gay.

There was a moment when I was in middle school when my sexuality came up in her presence. At that time in my life, I was the tallest in my class, very skinny, very effeminate. My classmates had already begun calling me "gay," but I didn't identify as such. Nor did I ever bring that information home.

One day I was driving with my mother to go pick up her new friend, Vernice, for lunch. Vernice had the same sun-kissed dark skin and booming voice as my mother, and like my mother, was born in the Caribbean. Jamaica, to be specific. When she and my mom were having a good time, they would slip into their respective accents, and to a stranger they might sound the same, but I could tell the difference between Trinidadian and Jamaican patois.

As soon as Vernice got in the car wearing her bright-colored jacket and African-print headwrap, she called me "handsome," which was a welcome ego boost. My mother drove off from the curb and we began our venture to lunch. I was sitting in the back seat, Vernice in the front passenger seat. She suddenly turned around, looked at me, and asked, "So, are you gay?"

Now, today we know this isn't the way to approach the subject of someone's sexuality. That said, Vernice's inquisition came off differently from how my classmates would approach the question. "Gay," coming out of her mouth, didn't have the same judgmental, biting tone. For Vernice, the answer to her query would be NBD. It was like she could see that I was carrying around this load and wanted to help me hold it. No one had been that generous with me about my sexuality, but I was still caught off guard.

"So, are you gay?" she said.

As my brain was about to formulate an answer, my mother interjected in a state of furious panic. "How could you say that?!" she replied for me. "How could you ask that?!"

I can still see the shock on my mother's face, her eyes blinking as her body recoiled in disbelief that Vernice had the audacity to ask what many already suspected.

At the time, I thought my mother's defensiveness was on my behalf, that she was protecting her son from the slanderous decree of others. (Trauma brain.) But if that were the case, my mother would know that a question like Vernice's wasn't slanderous. It wasn't cause to bare her claws. If anything, it was a chance for her to create a safety net for me to reveal something sacred about myself, an opportunity to reassure me that no matter what anybody said or did, I was loved. I was enough. I was *not* a sin.

But instead she responded as though she'd been captured and forced to watch the house of her dreams burn. She was in denial.

When I was growing up, my mother would say repeatedly, "I'm raising a strong Black man for a strong Black woman." She'd say these words to me and my grandma and her friends. "I'm raising a strong Black man for a strong Black woman." She'd say it in seriousness, with joy and pride. "I'm raising a strong Black man for a strong Black woman." I never interpreted that to mean "I don't want a gay child." But I've since learned that sometimes it's what people *don't* say that cuts the deepest. I couldn't articulate my feelings as a kid, but she'd drawn up plans for my life without consulting me, and I was expected to follow without question.

Nevertheless, when Vernice asked the question, denial was no match for the truth. Suddenly, my mother and I were both living in reality. I might be *gay*. And after Vernice asked her question, there was a choice that my mother had to make. And she made the wrong one. She chose to validate her own worldview as opposed to being there for her son.

I gave up my dreams of teaching to become an actor like my

mother, partially in hopes that it would bond us forever. My dad wasn't in the picture, and most of the kids I was around didn't care for me, so my mother was truly my world. Somewhere inside my young heart, I must have known that something about me could cause her to slip away—cause us to lose one another—and following in her footsteps was my way of keeping that from happening. That doesn't mean I regret becoming an actor or that my love for the stage isn't real, but a desire to please my mom was there as well.

Fast-forward to adulthood. At twenty-four years old, things were different for me. I identified proudly as gay and could no longer try to fulfill the role of being "a strong Black man for a strong Black woman."

My mother couldn't accept or respect my choice, which meant I had to "kick her to the curb." But how do you kick your mom to the curb? It's unsettling to even write. It's *icky*. The hairs on my arms stand up at the thought.

My mother is a powerhouse Black woman who raised me as a single parent and supported us off a career she made as an actress long before we were using hashtags to raise awareness about the ways in which Black performers have been unfairly kept out of Hollywood. She's an inspiration. An icon. A queen. And my hero. Before Oprah, I was loyal to my mother. Before any romantic love, or friendship love, there was my mother's love. My actual first love. How do you set boundaries with your first love when all you want is their acceptance and validation? Well, I think that's exactly why we *don't* set boundaries. Because we fear we'll lose those ABVs. But somehow I knew losing myself would be worse.

In the face of that fear, I tried to set up rules, asking my mother not to bring up my sexuality in a genuine attempt to keep our relationship intact and keep the peace. To keep her atop the pedestal that I'd always had for her. To keep seeing her as the superhero I always thought she was (and sometimes still pretend she is).

Every individual (even a child) has the right to set boundaries about what they like and don't like and how they wish to be treated. When someone expresses their boundaries to you, it's important not to get defensive or assert your opinion about whether their perspective is valid. It's important to respect their boundaries the same way you'd want someone to respect your own, even if it's your child. *Especially* if it's your grown child. Yes, you can have curious conversations about someone's boundaries if they're willing to discuss—not with the intention to change their mind but rather for deeper understanding so that you can show up for them fully.

I think boundaries are an act of love. Setting boundaries says, "I want to be in this relationship with you, but I want to make sure it stays safe so that we can both thrive in this union we share."

After about four months of failed attempts at establishing boundaries, I ended up cutting my mother off. I don't write that with pride; I write it with every ounce of pain my body can hold. The severing of our relationship didn't consist of a formal phone call or email or an argument. I just stopped picking up or responding to messages. If I did respond to a text, my message was short. My mother loved to send Bible verses in the morning, and I might respond, "Thank you." Eventually I wouldn't send anything, and it would rile her up, spurring her to send messages in which she called me "selfish" or "disrespectful" or "arrogant." Eventually I wouldn't send anything back, because I felt like I was putting myself in the line of fire every time we communicated. Who chooses to walk into a lion's den over and over and over, hoping not to be eaten alive? Me, apparently, at least for a little while. But enough was enough.

I had a choice to make—either live my life authentically or be my mother's obedient child. I chose the first. Honestly, it wasn't even a choice, because I was never going back into the closet. I was never going to repent for being my beautiful gay self. And I wasn't going to continue subjecting myself to my mother's ridicule.

To this day, ending communication with my mother was the hardest decision I've ever made. To choose my sanity and heart over her, to suddenly feel like a single balloon floating in the air, belonging to no one...I don't wish that on anyone. But I do wish you a joyous life in which your identity is celebrated and loved without condition. And if that creates conflict with the ideologies of your neighborhood, your friends, or your parents—then yes, they gotta go. It doesn't have to be forever, or completely. I love my mother deeply and still have hope that we'll be able to reunite and she'll be able to meet my husband and my puppy and be an integral part of my life again. But I'm not holding my breath. After a decade, I've made peace with it, because the enormous life I have wouldn't be possible if I'd shrunk and hidden myself to maintain her approval.

At the same time I lost communication with my mother, I actually gained my mentor, Ellen. I was working on writing my very first television script but genuinely had no idea what I was doing. A classmate of mine read one of my drafts and thought that his best friend's mother, Ellen, would be able to help me get it into shape. Ellen is a formidable actress and writer who had a wonderful career and now spends her time as an acting/writing coach and member of a theater company based not too far away from her home.

One afternoon, I met Ellen at her apartment in Chelsea, in an unassuming building on a quiet street. I can't quite explain it, but on some of those streets in downtown New York (especially in Chelsea or the Village), the sunlight hits the neighborhood differently, creating a picturesque oasis. Ellen's block was like that. I would turn off the main avenue, leaving the ruckus of buses, taxis, and people, and enter a different world.

When I got up to Ellen's door, she swung it open and embraced me with her signature mama-bear hug.

"What can I feed you?" she asked immediately. She always joked that as a Jewish mother, it was her duty to feed anyone who walked through her doors.

She sat me down at her gorgeous wooden dining table, which was right outside of her kitchen. Within minutes, there was a board of cookies, crackers, and different kinds of jam and spreads, and tea brewing. I don't love tea (I know, I'm a weirdo), but the way Ellen prepared it, with such love and tenderness, I could never refuse a cup. Once we were comfortable, we started talking about the script, and she very bluntly said, "It needs a lot of work."

After two hours of discussing the script—which was about a wildly successful gay Black actor who had a very public mental breakdown while trying to keep the news of his pending divorce under wraps (girl, what was I going through?)—Ellen said, "I'd like to help you with this."

To give some context, I started writing my script back in 2009, shortly after graduating NYU and before meeting Ellen. Queerness, and Black Queerness, weren't very visible in the zeitgeist. Like me, Ellen believed in the power of storytelling to move culture forward. Even if something doesn't exist, can we create it? It was exciting to have someone see my vision not just on paper, but in the world.

I agreed to Ellen's help, and so I went to her house weekly and we worked painstakingly on the story, the dialogue, the action lines. I'd never worked like that before, but it was essentially a free writing bootcamp. Obviously, working that hard on something that's so intimate and personal created space for us to share about our own lives.

When I shared what had happened with my mother, Ellen held my broken heart. Though she hated that I wasn't talking to my mother, being a mother herself, she also knew that I had to make that choice. And then she offered me a gift of wisdom. She said, "If you were your own parent, what advice would you give to yourself?" She impressed upon me that there was a baby Brandon inside of me who was grieving and hurting, who needed to be nurtured and comforted. He was going through something excruciating. Tragic. Sad. And I could keep ignoring that or I could take care of him. I could take care of me.

When I got home that night, I went up to my bedroom and pulled my journal from a shelf. I'd been writing in those Moleskines that have the squared graph paper. I sat at the foot of my bed and began to ponder the question Ellen had posed. After a few moments, I heard my advice clearly. First, I wrote: *I promise you'll be okay. I promise you'll get through this. I promise this will not destroy you.* Then I wrote: *What do you want out of life? Not just your career, but love, family, health, spirit. Focus on that. Get that. Make it your mission to get what you want out of this glorious life. If you want to change the world, then fucking change it. Change it for you and for anyone like you.* Finally, I wrote the most important thing of all: *I love you. You're not bad. You're not a disgrace. You're not a sin. And I love you. I love you so much.*

I don't know if I knew how to fully process any of it in the moment, but it's what I needed to hear. You don't have to wait for someone to affirm you; you can affirm yourself. In fact, what you say to yourself is far more important than what anyone else has to say. But remember, affirming yourself comes in the form of both words and actions. You deserve to be treated with respect and unconditional love, so never apologize for setting boundaries that reflect your valuable worth.

As for me and my mother, while writing this, the relationship is still strained. I'm actively, albeit slowly, working on finding the courage to see if there's a new set of boundaries that we can set with each other. I'm actively trying to give up the image I have of what our relationship used to be in order to make space for a new kind of relationship. A new possibility. But in all honesty, I don't want to. I want my best friend back. I want what we had, or more specifically, what I thought we had.

I'm also trying to safely see life through her eyes and perspective while not excusing the harm she's done. There's a poem by Jasmine Mans and part of it goes, "Tell me about the girl my mother was, before she traded in all her girl to be my mother." I sit with that sentiment a lot. What were her traumas? What was her resilience? What's been her healing? *Has* there been healing?

My therapist said of my mother's homophobia that if a person was diagnosed with bipolar disorder or some ailment that alters their psyche, someone on the receiving end of their outbursts could be more forgiving because they understand the issue isn't the person, it's the mental illness. Homophobia isn't an illness per se, but I think my therapist was encouraging me to remember that should homophobic rhetoric come forth in the rebuilding of our relationship, I don't have to take it personally. That perhaps I can find a way to metaphorically blame it on the "illness" so that I can find the strength to move forward.

Sounds like a whole lot of resilience will be needed to get to the necessary healing. I don't know if I have it in me. But for the first time with my mom, I want to, so that's a start.

If God had wanted me otherwise,

he would have created me otherwise.

—JOHANN VON GOETHE

---

8. Author's Note: Boundaries

Well, I already broke the rule around Author's Notes once, so I might as well do it again. Besides, the whole purpose of this book is to explore what it means to live beyond societal rules, and I think that includes book norms as well.

I've talked about having boundaries and admitted that when I was younger I may not have always known how to create them in the healthiest or clearest way. But I'm much better at it these days, so I wanted to offer some helpful steps for establishing your own.

I know that, for some of us, voicing our boundaries can make us feel uncomfortable, especially those of us who are people pleasers. It requires us to be vulnerable and honest about something we don't like. That level of honesty might get in our head about being perceived as "difficult," "mean," or "too sensitive." You're none of those things. You're someone who cares about both your mental and emotional well-being. You also care about the relationships you're in and want them to be successful. Success comes from vulnerability and honesty. Suffering and resentment come from staying silent and "rolling with the punches." You're worthy of your relationships being safe spaces. As you get used to defining your boundaries, and you experience the freedom, liberation, and safety that come from having them, I promise you'll get more confident in establishing them.

Also, sharing your boundaries with someone doesn't have to be a fight or argument. You can express them lovingly without compromising your integrity or shrinking yourself. Alright, here we go!

1. **Identify the problematic behavior you're trying to protect yourself from.**

   Example: My mother calls my sexuality a "choice" and continues to express that she prays for me to marry a woman.

   Sometimes identifying the problematic behavior can be a challenge to articulate. If that's the case, consider journaling, meditation, or chatting with someone you love and trust to gain clarity.

2. **Identify why that behavior is problematic for you.** There could be a multitude of reasons, including that it triggers past trauma, doesn't align with your values, and/or makes you feel worthless.

   Example: Calling my sexuality a "choice" and praying for me to marry a woman invalidates my identity, dismisses the truth of who I am, and disrespects what I want for myself. It's also hurtful.

3. **Ask yourself: What about the behavior would you like to change or shift for you to feel safe?** Another way to think about this is, if you could wave a magic wand and change the interactions from harmful to healthy, how would they look? How would they feel? What would be different, and what would remain the same? This line of questioning will lead you to naming the boundary.

> Example: I would like for my sexuality to be accepted by my mother. If that's not possible, then, at the very least, I would like for it to not be discussed.

> Now that we know what the boundary is, it's time to implement it.

4. **Be transparent with the person you want to create the boundary with by expressing how their behavior makes you feel.**

> Example: "It hurts me when you call my sexuality a choice."/ "It's infuriating when you say you want me to marry a woman."/ "The way you speak about my sexuality is disrespectful and invalidates my identity."

> *Sometimes it's challenging to express ourselves in the moment and face-to-face with the person, so I think it's perfectly acceptable to share your feelings in a letter, email, or text. Even if you choose to tell the person your boundary face-to-face or on the phone, writing it out ahead of time can be helpful in determining the language you want to use.*

5. **Set the boundary by asking for what you need.** Remember that magic wand? Use what you discovered in that

exploration to help articulate to the person what you'd like your interactions to look and feel like.

> Example: "I want nothing more than for you to accept and celebrate who I am, but at the very least I would appreciate if you didn't discuss my sexuality with me any longer."

Note, when we set a boundary, we hope that the person will receive and respect it immediately, but sometimes people don't. Oftentimes they get defensive. Usually it's because they interpret our request as an attack on their character or as us calling them a "bad person." We can remind them very directly that our request is not an attack on their character, and because we value the relationship, we want to share what we need from them. We don't need to justify our boundaries with excuses, but if the person is curious, we can engage in thoughtful dialogue to further help them understand the necessity of said boundary.

6. **Confirm your boundary has been heard and understood.** This is helpful to make sure that you and the person are indeed on the same page, and they understand what's being asked of them moving forward.

> Example: YOU: "So can we agree that moving forward you won't talk about my sexuality?" THEM: "Yes."

If someone is unwilling to honor your boundary, you have every right to adjust how or if you interact with them. Consider your psychological, physical, and spiritual safety as you establish what the adjustment might look like. Also know there are a myriad of ways your interaction with the person can take form. There's not a one-size-fits-all approach. You kind of have to be a "boundary tailor," if you will. You could decide there will be no contact at all. Perhaps it's contact only by phone for a predetermined amount of time. It could be that the amount of contact remains the same, but if the problematic behavior arises, you'll end the conversation. Determining how you interact with the person after establishing your boundary will likely be trial and error. That's totally okay! It's allowed to evolve and change as you see fit.

As you think about what is right for you, listen to how it feels in your body. Even if a boundary you're considering feels uncomfortable to say out loud or even to enact, does the thought of it bring an inkling of relief? Is your breathing a little deeper? Remember the gray space—two things get to coexist. You can feel sadness for needing to create the boundary, and also feel comfort in knowing that you no longer have to engage with behavior that hurts you. You can love a person and still restrict how much access they have to you.

Now, should the person agree to your boundary, then I think **gratitude** is a beautiful thing to express if you feel compelled to. Even though we're the ones establishing a boundary against behavior that may harm us, we're also operating under the assumption that the person didn't recognize their behavior was harmful. If they had known the ways in which it was triggering us, we trust they wouldn't have done it. Now that they are aware and they've agreed to do better, we can honor that growth in our relationship with a simple yet impactful "Thank you." "Thank you for hearing me and agreeing to honor my boundary."

No matter what, your mental and emotional well-being is of the utmost importance. You do not have to make or keep space in your life for those who don't value that. Value yourself enough to create boundaries wherever and whenever needed.

Boundaries are the distance at which I can love you and me simultaneously.

—PRENTIS HEMPHILL

---

9. Life Is Hard. We All Deserve Help.

MY FRIEND CARLIS, A HANDSOME BLACK MAN with a subtle Southern accent and great style, joined me for a gay night out in West Hollywood, where we ran into an old acquaintance of mine. You know those acquaintances whom you adore but for whatever reason the relationship just never develops into an actual friendship? There could be a ton of reasons that happens, be it where you both live, your schedules, or in this case, how you became acquaintances.

As I was introducing the acquaintance to Carlis, I wanted to share with Carlis how we knew each other, but I couldn't quite remember. So I said to him, "Wait, how did we meet?" He replied, "Oh, we met because of..." Then from out of his mouth came the name of my ex-boyfriend. It made me think of the scene in the first *Sex and the City* movie (the only *SATC* movie we acknowledge) where, after Mr. Big stands Carrie up at the altar, she goes to Mexico with the girls on what was supposed to be her honeymoon and one of the resort waiters calls her "Mrs. Preston" (Big's last name). Carrie turns to the girls and says, "Well, that was like taking a bullet." That's exactly how I felt as I heard my ex's name.

The thought of my ex always rattles me, because our relationship was such a defining chapter in my life. He transformed me as a person and is a key part of why I am the way I am now. Why I love the way I love, and why (speaking in my New York accent) "I don't fucks with everybody."

I lost myself in that man and lost so much in general. And yet I also gained so much, because that relationship forced me to learn many things. But some lessons you only need to learn once. Emotional abuse is one of them.

I wasn't sure if I was going to write about this, because part of me is still protective of my ex, who we'll continue to call Kevin—yes, the same Kevin I've mentioned a few times now.

Many of those who've been in any kind of abusive relationship can relate to that feeling of protectiveness. The logical brain that knows your abusive partner is scum for the way that they abused you. The PTSD brain that still sees the non-abusive version of the partner you fell in love with. There's still a tether of loyalty that I have to him. There's also a level of blame that I put on myself for getting into that relationship and staying in it for as long as I did.

I want to write about this, not to rake him over the coals or even to hold him accountable. Honestly, whatever he's doing and wherever he is, I genuinely wish him well, though I also wish him never to come anywhere near me for as long as we both are on this physical plane. (Tu-huh!) But I'm going to write about this so that you understand a bit more about this piece of my journey toward loving myself, and I hope that if you recognize aspects of this relationship in your own situation or the situation of someone you know, you'll find the tenacity to leave. That said, I want to also acknowledge there are so many reasons as to why abused partners stay, be it financial or familial (having kids) or something else. I recognize that ending abuse can sometimes be complicated. Very complicated.

Though we didn't date until after I graduated, I actually met Kevin my junior year of college. He was a tall, skinny brown boy with a handsome face and a smile that immediately excited me emotionally and sexually. He was two years older than me, so that was also appealing. (I've always had a thing for older guys, even if it's just by a month.) Though he'd already graduated a year prior, he was working on the school production I was in as an assistant director.

One time he was adjusting my costume during a fitting, and his grip was gentle but strong. He was meticulous about details, which I thought was so sexy. And when I think someone is sexy, I sweat. Like a lot. I get so nervous and flustered and clammy. I think at one point I was fidgeting, trying to wipe my sweaty forehead, and he firmly said, "You need to hold still." I obeyed his orders while getting aroused, but I didn't act on my crush because I had only been out of the closet for a couple months at that point.

Two years later, I graduated and ran into Kevin at a party. We chatted for a bit and then he said, "We should get dinner sometime."

"Okay!" I said. We exchanged numbers and I forgot all about it. I didn't believe he genuinely found me attractive or was actually asking me out. As we've discussed, I never believed people found me attractive, as I felt undesirable because of my dark skin, femness, and gynecomastia. But to my surprise, he texted me a week later and we went on a date. It was the start of an almost two-year relationship.

In the beginning, I couldn't get enough of him. He was so smart and thoughtful, and he made me laugh. And the sex was unbelievable. I felt loved by him, and unlike the white boy, Pinky, from a few years earlier, this was unapologetic love. He was protective of me and wanted to involve me in every area of his life. I'd never felt so wanted. Within the first two weeks, I met his closest friends and even met his dad, who happened to be visiting New York. We were on top of the world. Some call it the honeymoon phase.

One night, about a month into dating, we were hanging with one of his best friends, who was in town from Los Angeles. She was fabulous, a respected costume designer, with big eyes and a bigger personality, and baby, she could turn a lewk. We'd all gone out that night and spent the evening laughing, drinking, and bonding. When it was time to go home, it was already planned that I was going to sleep over at Kevin's place and, if I remember correctly, the best friend would stay in the living room. So we squeezed into a yellow cab and made our way back downtown. Being that we're all in theater and film, we were discussing a show, and I offered an opinion that differed from Kevin's. What I said didn't feel like a big deal, just a different opinion, but Kevin got pissed. So pissed he stopped speaking. To me. He would still answer his best friend, but it was as if I was no longer there. The best friend called him out on his behavior, but he wouldn't budge. In fact, he doubled down and stopped speaking to her as well.

I apologized to him profusely. No response. I tried to take back my opinion and agree with his point. No response. I tried to hold his hand. He pulled it away.

At the time, I was living at home in Queens, and even during the day, when the trains and buses are running on time, it would take at least an hour or an hour and a half to get back to my place. It being well after midnight meant it wasn't really an option for me to travel to Queens, and my stuff was already at his place. We went to his apartment, got ready for bed, and lay there next to each other. Finally, he started talking to me again. I felt a relief. I apologized again, and we had sex.

I realize now the downward spiral of our relationship was gradual, unnoticeable until it was unbearable. But I look back and I see these red flags that should have clued me in to the inevitable. Maya Angelou says, "When someone shows you who they are, believe them the first time." I should have known that a person who's willing to ignore me for hours because I disagreed with their opinion about a show is not someone I should be with. But I was young and in love, so instead I moved in with him. (Cue laugh track.)

Apart from that night, we were usually good. And now living together, we were both eager to play house and make the space our home.

Our relationship was before the legalization of same-sex marriage. I didn't grow up in a world where I ever imagined that I could openly live with a man whom I was in love with, yet here I was doing just that, and I was willing to put up with a lot to protect this unspoken dream.

But slowly, he began his silent treatments once again. Sometimes I knew why—maybe I did or said something he disagreed with, or maybe I was running late in meeting him and he felt awkward waiting. Other times I had no idea what set him off. Either way, the bouts of silence were longer than that first time in the cab. They could last all day. Kevin would come into the apartment or leave without saying a word, not responding to my questions or my texts until he was ready. I found myself always doing my best not to upset him, because if I wasn't getting the silent treatment, I was on the receiving end of full-on yelling.

He soon started to have a problem with the people I was hanging out with, including my closest male friends. We might go out to dinner or dancing with some of those friends, and either on the way there or afterward, he would express how much he didn't like them, calling my peeps "arrogant" or "cocky." (As I recount this, it's not lost on me that "arrogant" was the word my mother used when she wanted to cut me down for setting boundaries. She and Kevin had major similarities.)

When he would disparage my friends, I never quite knew what to say. Obviously, he was threatened by them; I can see that now. But at the time, I would get a pit in my stomach and question my judgment because he was so confident in his analysis. I also didn't want to argue, because arguing never ended well, so I mostly just feigned agreement. But they were my friends and I loved them, and I would hang out with them anyway at the expense of dealing with his nasty temper when I got home. After a while, though, the stress wasn't worth it. So I only hung out with the people he liked.

Then there were the times we'd be out and he would get upset at me for some unknown reason and just leave. Obviously, the plan was to be out together, so I wouldn't take my key, because he had his. I'd go to the doorman, and with a big smile say, "I locked myself out and I think Kevin is sleeping. Can I borrow the spare?"

As a result, I stopped leaving my keys at home, because I never knew what would set him off.

There were times when he would say something hurtful or condescending to me in the corner of a party and then a second later be smiling and laughing with his friends. There were the times where I would have to be home by a certain time if I didn't want to deal with his wrath. There were times he would accuse me of cheating, yelling at me for my supposed betrayal, completely enraged. His anger tore through our household and abolished all the trust and love we'd built between us. Emotionally, I shut down. I felt helpless, unsure of how to quiet the beast. Eventually I found myself preemptively having sex with him as a way to calm him down before he could get angry yet again. And sometimes he would give me thoughtful gifts to make up for his irrational tirades.

I gave up my agency because if I didn't, I was punished. To be with someone who continuously builds you up and cuts you down while you never know when either will happen is unsafe, a terrible emotional roller coaster. One night, when he was out of town, I got to hang out with my two best friends—Ismael, a sharp-tongued, openhearted Black Puerto Rican who always speaks his mind, and Fernando, a six-foot-two Dominican Queer from New Jersey who's the definition of fabulous. After a night of dancing and drinking, we decided to get some late-night eats at the restaurant Cafeteria in Chelsea. (They make a goooood mac and cheese.) Once we were full, we ventured back out on Sixth Avenue, where we got on the topic of Kevin. Ismael said that Kevin wasn't good for me. "He dims your light!" In that moment, something came over me and I pushed Ismael.

I don't push people. I don't fight. That type of behavior was beyond out of character for me. But Ismael squared up, because that push was a starter. Fernando, taller than both me and Ismael, physically stepped in between the two of us. (Note: I think it's important to say that Ismael is more than a best friend; he's my brother. We love and fight like brothers, and our early twenties consisted of a lot of growing and healing with each other.) I was so protective of my relationship to Kevin, and of Kevin himself. Deep down, I knew he was toxic, but I didn't think I could do any better. If you believe that one person is your only shot at love for the rest of your life, the stakes become very high. Too high.

Almost a year into us living together, my grandmother passed away. And then I distanced myself from my mother after she became vocal about my "lifestyle choices" being a sin. Essentially, I lost my family. Kevin was now my only family, and I felt like I had to make our relationship work because I didn't want to be alone. *And* I was a struggling artist with more jobs than I could count and more credit card debt than I cared to admit, which basically meant I was unable to take care of myself. Moving back to a homophobic household with my mother wasn't an option, so I was dependent on Kevin in a variety of ways, which he was well aware of.

I was in hell, but I thought it was my fault. I believed I was causing him to get frustrated, and so if I could get my shit together, he would be better.

While I was adjusting to this cage I found myself in, I was seeing my mentor, Ellen, a few times a week. I can honestly say that she's the one who helped me begin unlocking my cage. In teaching me how to be a better writer, she taught me how to have a voice. The more time I spent with Ellen, the stronger my point of view became, because she would ask questions that only someone who's been on the earth for a certain amount of time can ask. She'd never give me the answer but taught me to trust that "little voice" we tell kids about when we're explaining intuition. When I spoke, she listened, and honored what I said. She was different from Kevin and different from my mother, both of whom preferred to tell me what I should believe. With Ellen, my true voice became stronger, my perspective clearer.

Ellen never spoke poorly about Kevin when I would share stories. Instead she spoke highly of me. She showed me my worth.

"Brandon, you're special."

"Brandon, you're talented."

"Brandon, you're gonna go far."

"Brandon, you've got the goods."

"Brandon, you're too good to settle."

The more worthy I felt, the less I was willing to be yelled at and tolerate Kevin's behavior. A shift began. When he bucked, I bucked right back. If he wanted to give me the silent treatment, I watched TV. If he gaslit me, I would say, "Go fuck yourself." He hated my new voice, and I hated him.

As I mentioned earlier, I don't hate people. And I rarely use the word "hate" in general, because of my grandma's insistence that it was too strong a word that only destroys you. Him, though, I hated. I hated how he treated me. I hated our home. I hated how much I depended on him. Most of all I hated how much I still loved him. I loved the way he pouted his lips to kiss me. I loved the way he caved his shoulders inward when he wanted to be the little spoon. I loved the way he would fawn over good theater. I loved when he snorted. I loved how comfortable he was in his femininity. I knew he was scared sometimes that it could put him in danger, but I admired how he continually forged ahead anyway, owning it. I loved how loyal he was to his friends and family. I loved how ambitious he was in telling Queer stories and collaborating with Queer POC artists. How could someone I loved so much also be someone who hurt me so much?

Tina Turner sang, "What's love got to do with it?" I understand that now, but back then I thought love should be everything. Like if we loved each other, why couldn't he just be as sweet as he was in those first few months? Why couldn't we laugh and fuck and chill like we used to? Why couldn't I just love him, and he love me, and that be enough?

My mother used to say, "Your friends are a reflection of you." If you've got friends who are loyal, kind, and good, then chances are you're that way too. If you've got friends who are rude, shady, and disrespectful—welp, you already know, boo. I think this is similar in romantic relationships, except your partners aren't so much a reflection of you as they are a reflection of your self-worth. We put up with a lot of bullshit in our romantic partnerships when, somewhere inside of us, we don't believe we are worth more. Deserve more. I think we also put up with BS based on our definition of love.

My definition of love was partially rooted in the fact that people had said the word to me without taking consideration of their actions. If someone said they loved me, I believed them and never called into question their behaviors. I personally adore Maya Angelou's take on love, so much so that it's tattooed on my chest: *Love liberates, it doesn't bind.*

Until this relationship, I hadn't internalized the phrase "Actions speak louder than words." But honey, they do. A love that traps and cages you isn't love. A love that patronizes you and disrespects you isn't love.

Looking back, I can see that I became a possession, something for Kevin to control. And for me, I based my worth on being with him. In reality, the only person who can give me my worth is me. If I'm not willing to see my value and own it, then I'll always find myself beholden to others, chasing worth in destructive souls. In fact, the first time Kevin ignored me in the back of the cab, I began the chase.

Hating him was the only way I knew how to stop running and free myself. Obviously, I know now that there are healthier ways to end things with someone, but in the cloud of the relationship, I wasn't processing...I was surviving. Hate became my key to get free, because my voice, though stronger, wasn't strong enough yet. Also, I can admit now that I was far more comfortable in the chaos of being together than in the unknown of being on my own.

I did leave once. I took my stuff and moved in with two of my friends, a married couple in Brooklyn. I was finally free of Kevin, but I missed him. We started talking, and he said he missed me as well. He was so sweet, like when we first met. Two weeks later, I moved back in.

We were better than ever when I moved back in. But as you can guess with abuse, that only lasted a few weeks, and then it was worse than ever, to the point that we mutually agreed that when our lease was up in the coming weeks, we would go our separate ways. For a month, we lived in the same home and slept in the same bed but began living separate lives. If you've ever cohabitated with someone after a breakup, it's not enjoyable. Rather, it's confusing, painful, and weird.

At the end of the month, there we were in our foyer, both standing by our suitcases. Behind us, our life was in boxes as we waited for the movers, both of us aware that this chapter of our lives was about to be over.

Multiple things being true is often harder to reckon with, in my opinion. It was true that I was relieved that this part of my life was coming to an end. It was true that no matter how much I hated him, I loved him still, deeply. And I was very scared to be without him. Maybe there was a part of me, with my overdrawn bank account, that was nervous about how I would make it on my own without his financial support. Of course, there was also a part of me that was scared to be without him because I didn't want to end up alone. But mostly I was scared to be without him because he was all I knew as a long-term lover, and he was all I wanted to know, if I'm being honest. In my Tyra Banks voice: "I was rooting for us!"

We looked at each other in that final moment. He was leaving first, and I was going to hang back and wait for one of my friends to come help me with my stuff. We hugged. Then we kissed. It took everything I had not to collapse into his arms, lose my shit, and declare, "Maybe we should give it another shot!"

We pulled back from each other and tried to smile. And then he was gone.

I felt like I was alone for the first time ever. Our relationship started literally right after I graduated college, and now I was standing in this emptied apartment. No school. No man. No mom. What was I about to embark on?

Professionally, I was pursuing a job in fitness, which was a welcome distraction. Personally, I strapped on all the armor I could find. I didn't want to feel. I didn't think it was safe for me to feel. I

buried myself in a variety of self-help techniques, including affirmations and journaling. I declared that I would never lose myself
for the love of a man. I would love myself. I would see myself and
not rely on a man to make me feel seen. I built up my confidence
unattached to others, which is important. But while doing so, I also
continued to block out the possibility that people could genuinely
like and be attracted to me, which meant somewhere inside, I still
thought I was the bottom of the barrel.

Two months after the split, I was rejecting people before they
could reject me. I was making a joke about myself before they
could make a joke about me. Or worse, I was fawning over guys
who weren't interested in me or were physically attractive but emotionally unavailable. The chase was still happening. I was always on
the verge of repeating with a new guy the same pattern I had with
Kevin. I may have built up my confidence, but it was all external—
lip service, with no real gravitas.

I had to acknowledge that my ex didn't create any new beliefs
about myself—he just exploited what was already there. He woke
me up to how weak my self-worth already was. I thought after our
split that I had to build my self-worth back. But in reality, it was
never there. I had to build it, period.

After my breakup, I was couch surfing for a while as I figured out
where I was going to end up and how I was going to afford wherever I ended up. During that time, I reconnected with an old friend
of my mother's who I hadn't seen since I was in middle school. I
called him Uncle Barry, a white gay man with impeccable taste and
a soft, therapeutic nature. I was obsessed with Uncle Barry, probably because he was the first person I knew who was openly gay.

He lived in a chic high-rise apartment overlooking the river on the West Side, filled with expensive furniture and Queer art. I couldn't verbalize it at my young, repressed age, but I wanted to be like Uncle Barry, surrounded by good taste and shirtless men.

Reuniting with him after over a decade was surreal. I never processed that one day I'd be a grown-up like him, and yet here we were, two adults. Two gay adults. It was like no time had passed, and I was beyond thrilled to share company with someone who'd meant so much to me in my childhood. I think that after the severed relationship with my mother, I longed for someone who had knowledge of my life before college, who knew me before I had any awareness or consciousness of adult life, who knew where I'd been and maybe could give me directions on where to go.

I told him everything. School. Career. Jobs. Grandma passing. Mother becoming born-again. My breakup. My couch-surfing living situation. He took it all in. Perhaps I expected him to say, "Poor baby, Uncle Barry's gotchu now," and move me into that highrise. To my dismay, he didn't. Instead he looked at me and asked, "Where are your friends?"

Odd question, I thought. But in retrospect, I met Uncle Barry when I was six or seven years old. The '90s. He was an out and proud gay man before *Will & Grace* and marriage equality, before (for better or worse) corporations sponsoring Pride. The decade before, the gay community had been ravaged by AIDS. I couldn't imagine the amount of friends Uncle Barry—and my mother, for that matter—had lost. Friends who loved and reaffirmed him and made it okay to be out and proud. And now it's 2011, and he's sitting across from twenty-three-year-old Queer me.

"Where are your friends?" he asked. "Do they know about all this?"

"Some of it, but not all," I answered.

"Why is that?"

"I don't want to be a burden."

Uncle Barry looked at me quizzically and asked, "Do you allow your friends to come to you when they're down?"

"Of course."

"And do you think they're a burden when they do?"

"No. Not at all," I exclaimed. "I'm glad they trust me."

"But you won't go to them?"

I shrugged my shoulders, unclear on what he was getting at.

"I have to tell you, that's manipulative," he said.

I was shocked. Manipulative?! I am many things, honey. Classy. Bougie. Ratchet (hey, Megan Thee Stallion!) and messy. But not manipulative. I said as much to him, and he gently said, "Allowing your friends to be able to need you but never letting yourself need them keeps all the power in your court. The relationship becomes one-sided and controlled by you. So it's manipulative."

Bitch, I tell you I was gagged choking on that truth. Like, Uncle Barry, you ain't have to DRAG me like that while I'm eating this steak and French fries (thatchu paying for)! But he was so right. Those people I called my best friends were in the dark and being kept at arm's length. Sure, part of that was the nature of my relationship to Kevin. You remember I told you I stopped hanging out with whomever he didn't approve of, which happened to be some of my besties. Abusers are smart in their ability to isolate you from those who could save you. But also, I didn't approach my friends because I wanted to maintain a façade of perfection, of having my shit together.

Rebuilding those relationships required asking for forgiveness.

I had to apologize that I let a relationship to this man I was with for just shy of two years become more important than the relationships I'd had with friends for upward of six or seven years. I also had to shake off my "manipulative" tendencies (even if they were unintentional) and be transparent about what I was dealing with. That was hard, embarrassing, and sad. And yet all of my friends showed up for me.

I believe the point my Uncle Barry was trying to make was that these weren't just my friends, they were my family. My chosen family.

The term "chosen family" is such a staple in the Queer community because so many of us have to redefine and rebuild our family after coming out of the closet. I use the term often, but I do have moments when I don't like it. I don't want "chosen" to ever imply that I might choose someone to be in my family one day and choose to kick them out the next, like some blood families do. But I know that's not what the term means. Being "chosen" is about intention. And if there's anything you know about me at this point, it's that I value intention.

When you hear Queer folx talk about their "chosen family," we're not just talking about friends with whom we brunch or chat on the phone, we're talking about people who saved us, who reaffirm us in a world that discards us.

So, if you have people in your life who're the roots of your tree, hold them close to your heart. Don't take them for granted. Honor your relationship with them, because it's a treasure. And if you haven't found your chosen family yet, don't worry. They're out there and are so excited to know you. As the saying goes, "You still haven't met all the people who are going to love you."

*   *   *

The last thing I'll write on this subject of my ex is that neither I nor my friends recognized just how toxic my relationship with Kevin was. We were young and didn't have the language. In fact, it wasn't until about six years after he and I broke up (which was about two years into my relationship with Matthew) that I was sitting in my car somewhere on an LA side street killing time on Instagram. I came across a carousel that said, "Ten Ways to Know You're in an Emotionally Abusive Relationship." I scrolled and identified nine of the ten signs in my relationship with Kevin.

The ten signs were:

> **Control** (for example, dictating what time I had to be home)
>
> **Yelling** (happened all the time)
>
> **Contempt** (responding to my desires with mean-spirited sarcasm, disgust, or apathy)
>
> **Excessive defensiveness** (often having a reaction if I asked if he needed help with something or if he was challenged in some way)
>
> **Stonewalling** (the silent treatment)
>
> **Blame** (being made to feel as though I was the reason for any unhappiness or discord)
>
> **Gaslighting** (My concerns were always wrong, or I was being dramatic, or "crazy." Full disclosure: As I'm writing this chapter, I'm still going, "Maybe it wasn't that bad, maybe I *am* being dramatic." Shit is deep.)
>
> **Isolation** (not hanging with my friends because it upset him)

Volatility (mood swings and outbursts followed by gifts)

The only sign I didn't identify with was **Threats**. But honestly, I'm sure threats were there in some form. Maybe Kevin wasn't threatening to hit me or throw me out of the house, but I never felt like I could make a decision without there being repercussions. Up until reading that carousel, I just thought it was a relationship that "didn't work out." I thought that maybe in a different time of our lives, the relationship could've worked. But the truth was more difficult and complex.

Upon this realization, I cried like I cried that day we said goodbye to each other. Having language to describe and validate my experience was almost too much, yet at the same time, it was very healing, allowing me to see that some of my fights or walls with Matthew had nothing to do with him and everything to do with this old, abusive relationship. Having the language allowed me to forgive myself, forgive Kevin, and show up as a fuller, more vulnerable partner with Matthew.

I included the signs above because maybe, had I seen this list all those years ago, I would have ended things with Kevin sooner, or at the very least would have understood that something beyond a bad romance was at play.

Also, I'd like to add that if you trust your friends about everything else in your life, trust them when they say the person you're dating is trash. If your friends are folx who genuinely have your back, there's no need for them to lie to you. They're seeing something that you may not be clocking because you've got your rose-colored glasses on. Or rather, your trauma glasses on.

If you recognize your relationship in anything I've described, reach out to a friend, family, or chosen family member. Let them help you.

Life is hard. We all deserve help.

**Stop chasing things that are beneath
the truth of who you are.**

—IYANLA VANZANT

FRIENDS

To have a person you aren't related to who loves you unconditionally, and you love them the same. They love you through your wins and losses and mistakes, and you love them the same. They love you without judgment, and you love them the same.

To have someone who knows the anatomy of your heart, but you're not romantic with them. They know the shape of your dreams. The coordinates of your fears. The remedy for your tears. The keys to your belly laughter. With just a call or a text, they know how to calm your doubts, banish your insecurities, and build your confidence.

Out of all the people in the world, you and this person just…click. Connect. Your energies just…

That's a gift.

10. Make It Home

THE OTHER DAY I WAS preparing to go to a restaurant in LA that I hadn't been to before. I planned to wear black jeans and a black sleeveless crop top but thought it wise to Google the restaurant and get a sense of the ambience. When I clicked on the restaurant's website, the homepage was a picture of the restaurant, and it was bougie AF. Wearing a sleeveless crop top might have been a little too casual, so I opened my closet and began reassessing my lewk for the evening. I've always loved clothes, something I no doubt inherited from my mother, who has impeccable style. She knew how to fuse elegance with streetwear and a touch of something quirky or special—be it a bold-print boot, a dramatic long coat, or denim jeans with fringe. Whatever she put together, bright colors could always be found.

I wasn't always as bold as her, but I could still clean up well. With my newly accepted gender identity of being nonbinary, I'd been reconsidering my relationship to clothes and how mostly male-gendered my wardrobe was. I wanted to give myself permission to play with more boldness and femininity like my mother. Hence the aforementioned crop top. My reckoning inadvertently opened a trap door of exploration toward my relationship to clothes, specifically in a Black body.

Admittedly, whenever I have to go somewhere really nice, be it a restaurant, someone's house, or a store, I tend to choose an outfit that does more than just signal that I Googled the dress code; I pick one that says, "I can afford to be here," i.e., "I belong here." When you've been mistaken for a server or salesclerk, ignored or denied service, or received as many dirty looks as I have from managers or patrons, you quickly learn that what you wear can be a way to avoid being disrespected. At least that's what I learned when I was way too young.

Before we dive into that, I want to acknowledge there's a valid argument to be made about dressing for others being toxic, especially if the goal is to move beyond the expectations of others. There's also a valid argument to be made about trying to guarantee one's safety by choosing to dress in a way that's accepted, and also a valid argument to be made about dressing in an expected or accepted way when one doesn't have the emotional capacity to navigate ignorance.

Oftentimes, in conversations of authenticity, some people judge "following the norms" or dressing differently than you might if you felt safe as being inauthentic. It's not as easy as that. This is yet another example of a gray area. What I tell others when it comes to matters of authenticity is to make whatever choice you want, but to just do it consciously. Making a conscious decision to follow a societal norm for work, a family function, a trip to a grocery store, or dinner at a bougie restaurant in a white neighborhood is different from blindly following it because you subconsciously think said norm is inherently, unquestionably right. And as you remain conscious, you'll build the capacity and the courage to ignore those norms and expectations more often, and maybe eventually altogether. But honor where you are on your journey. Easy on the judgment.

As for learning how to use clothes in order to signal "I can afford to be here"—well, I acquired that baggage young, because I had a minister grandmother and an actress mother. They were public figures in their respective communities and careers, so presentation for these two professional Black women was of utmost importance. But for me it took on a life of its own in 2001.

Let's circle back to my youth once again. That September, I was about a month into my freshman year at a boarding high school in Rome...Georgia. Apart from it being a culture shock, I was also navigating being away from home and being in a new school, a new city, one where most everyone I saw was white. This was a stark difference from my international middle school in Queens and the melting pot of New York City. Eleven days into the month, I was sitting in study hall when one of my "dorm brothers," a white skater kid with the same name as me, entered the classroom and exclaimed in a hushed panic, "A plane hit one of the Twin Towers!" After an excruciating day of not being able to get ahold of my mother, I finally made contact and had confirmation that my family was safe. Things in Georgia went back to normal pretty much right away, so perhaps I naively expected to experience something similar when I returned to New York in November for my Thanksgiving holiday break.

New York was quieter than usual, as the city was still in mourning. Even though I spent most of the time nestled in my Queens neighborhood far away from downtown Manhattan, the fear was palpable and the grief was overwhelming. The city and country were hyperfocused on reigniting patriotism, rebuilding our security, and "catching terrorists," so I never expected in the midst of all of that, I would experience being followed in a store for the first time.

As I understand it, being followed by security, police, or any authority is an experience that is mostly reserved for Black and brown folx. It's something that, from what I've gathered after attending PWIs for most of my educational career and working among mostly white folx in my professional endeavors, most white people rarely experience. Having attended private school since I was a toddler, perhaps I thought this fucked-up rite of passage wouldn't befall me. Somewhere inside, I must have thought I skipped that chapter of life because when it happened, it felt like a joke. For that, I blame the Disney Channel.

Wait, hear me out.

When I was younger, the Disney Channel was my life. I'll never forget the day we got it. I was sitting at home, as I usually did, on the steps under the archway that separated our living room from the dining room. A thirteen-inch TV sat on top of a small plastic stand, painted to look like marble. Most of the time the TV was tilted toward the dining room, because I preferred to sit on the steps, inches away from it, as opposed to being on one of the couches that were feet away. My grandmother would periodically look in from the kitchen and insist, "Brandon, ya too close to de TV! You'll go blind! Scoot back, child." I would begrudgingly move a couple inches away until she was satisfied, and then once she was back in the kitchen, I would return to my original spot.

If it were comfortable, I would have watched TV with my nose pressed to the glass. I've always wanted to *feel* what was happening on-screen. Even today, my husband periodically begs me to lower the volume on our TV, because my love of being immersed in a good show still prevails.

One evening, while my grandmother was in the kitchen, no doubt preparing a curry chicken with vegetable fried rice, I was in my spot on that step watching something on one of the local stations—probably a favorite syndicated sitcom like *Family Matters* or *The Fresh Prince of Bel-Air.* I heard the screen door open, and since it was nearly dinnertime, I knew it was my mother. I quickly moved myself back from the TV to an acceptable position. A moment later, the front door opened. My mother floated in, beaming.

"Turn on channel 49," she exclaimed.

"Why?" I asked.

"Just do it."

I grabbed the remote and did as I was told. There he was. My icon. My king. My reason for being. Mickey Mouse. My mother had added Disney to our cable package.

Apart from Oprah, I was a Disney junkie. I had *Fantasia* and *Disney's Sing-Along Songs: The Twelve Days of Christmas* on VHS, which I watched to exhaustion. But nothing compared to *101 Dalmatians.* (We only acknowledge the animated version here.) I never tired of watching Pongo and Perdita outsmart evil diva Cruella De

Vil to pull off an epic rescue of all those puppies—not to mention I had the deepest connection to Rolly, the Dalmatian pup with a little extra weight, who, in the middle of being kidnapped, still managed to let it be known, "I'm hungry, Mother. I'm hungry." Honestly, my soul mate.

I would have been happy to keep watching all my videotapes, but with a whole channel dedicated to everything Disney, I could finally pledge my allegiance 24/7: *DuckTales, Kids Incorporated,* and, of course, my favorite, *The Mickey Mouse Club.* (We only acknowledge the seasons pre–Justin, Christina, and Britney here.) This was a true game changer in my after-school and weekend living.

In addition to the exhilarating TV shows, there would also be movies and specials that coincided with a holiday, like *Halloweentown* or *The Muppet Christmas Carol.* When MLK Day rolled around, there was this special (I don't remember the name of it or much of the plot, tbh) that featured a diverse group of kids learning about racism. About midway through, there's a scene where one of the white boys—let's call him Petey—experiences being Black in the Jim Crow South. They showed this by switching out the white child actor with a Black child actor, but the audience was to understand it was the same character. So Black Petey enters a convenience store, and as he begins shopping, he finds himself being followed by the store clerk, an older white man. It's a tense scene, and as the clerk is about to confront him in one of the aisles, Black Petey runs toward a Black woman who plays the magical narrator of the special. In his fear, he hugs her, which turns him back into his white self. The store clerk instantly leaves him alone. (Trust, it's not lost on me that the narrator who saved the white boy was a Black woman, or that he returned to whiteness upon hugging her. Though I could now talk ad nauseam about the use of the "magical negro" trope in media or the ways in which Black women are always expected to save everyone, at the time of the special, I wasn't old enough to be aware of any of these dynamics.)

For me, seeing a Black child my age being chased in a convenience store by a grown-ass white man was terrifying, but being a '90s baby, I thought, *Wow, it's crazy how that* used to *happen to Black people.* (Cue the laugh track here.) I can see now that was probably the intention of this special—to boast to us children how far our country has come and remind us how lucky we were to live in a "post-racial America." Lies, obviously, but I gobbled up every last crumb, and that's why, years later, when I found myself being followed at my neighborhood Walgreens, it felt like a joke. I looked around for a statuesque Black woman to run and hug, hoping she could jolt me out of this nauseating prehistoric reality. But there was no woman to hug. This wasn't the past, and it was certainly no joke.

It was wintertime in New York, which is brutal, so I was bundled up in a hoodie underneath a winter coat, long johns underneath jeans, and classic light brown Timberland boots—the latter being a staple in many Black New Yorkers' closets. I walked into the store like I always did. A security guard was standing by the doorway as one always did. He was a little bit taller than me with a salt-and-pepper beard, and I believe he was of South Asian descent, which honestly made the whole thing even more of a mindfuck. Someone like him was already under scrutiny with the racist propaganda being perpetuated post-9/11 that anyone brown, Muslim, or "Muslim-looking" (whatever that means) was a terrorist. I gave him one of those straight-boy head nods that I learned from my cousins and proceeded to the pharmacy to pick up a prescription for my grandmother, which wasn't ready yet.

It had been a twenty-minute walk to Walgreens, so there was no way I was going back home. I decided to kill time in the store by checking out the magazine aisle. Since this Walgreens was in a predominantly Black neighborhood, they carried "urban" magazines like *Word Up!* and *Black Hair*. I would find myself totally transfixed by the elaborate hairdos donned by the Black women modeling, wishing I was allowed to try a few of them out myself. After a couple minutes of gawking, I noticed out of the corner of my eye someone standing at the end of the aisle. When I looked up, I saw the security guard.

I didn't think anything of it and went back to perusing my magazine. Then I remembered that I was out of my favorite shampoo at the time—Head & Shoulders. (Hold your judgment.)

I put the magazine down and went to the toiletries aisle. As I was browsing, looking for the bottle I wanted, I again noticed out of the corner of my eye someone standing at the end of the aisle. It was the security guard again. And still I thought nothing of it. I found the bottle I was looking for, grabbed it, and decided to go back to the magazines. When I got there, the guard was already standing at the end of the aisle.

This time, I felt him waiting. Watching. I couldn't for the life of me understand what he was waiting for or what had piqued his interest so much. I glanced down the other end of the aisle, looking for something or someone who was a potential threat. But there was no one. Just me. Then I remembered that scene from the Disney Channel.

As a Taurus, my stubbornness took hold, and I refused to believe this man was following me. I had to make sure this was actually happening, so I went to another aisle. As you might guess, there he was. Standing at the end. So I went to *another* aisle. There he was. Standing at the end. Waiting. Watching. It was like some kind of Charlie Chaplin lazzo.

A joke.

Finally, I accepted the reality of what was happening, and an electric shock went through my body. I was enraged.

In 2020, I did an interview on my podcast *Black Folx* with life coach Pervis Taylor. In our discussion about rage, he said that underneath anger is sadness, but people often choose anger because it makes them feel empowered. Looking back, yes, I was desperate to reclaim my power, the power that came from knowing that I was an honest and good kid. A power that was taken from me the moment that security guard made a judgment based on my Black skin. I can also recognize that underneath that anger, my heart was broken. It was official. I was now fourteen, and my childhood was dead.

As much as teenagers might protest this idea, they're still children who're learning, evolving, making mistakes. But Black children don't have the privilege of mistakes or holding on to their innocence.

According to a 2014 article in the *Journal of Personality and Social Psychology* titled "The Essence of Innocence: Consequences of Dehumanizing Black Children," psychologists found that, beginning at age ten, Black boys are more likely than their white peers to be misperceived as older, to be viewed as guilty of suspected crimes, and to face police violence if accused of a crime. Similarly, *Girlhood Interrupted: The Erasure of Black Girls' Childhood*, a report from Georgetown Law Center on Poverty and Inequality, found that adults view Black girls as "less innocent and more adult-like than their white peers, especially in the age range of 5–14." These statistics are alarming, infuriating, and devastating. They also track.

In 2014, in Cleveland, a twelve-year-old by the name of Tamir Rice was playing with a toy gun when an officer shot and killed him. In 2015, in Texas, after receiving reports of kids jumping the fence of a neighborhood pool, a white police officer slammed a fifteen-year-old Black girl in a bathing suit to the ground, then drew his gun on the unarmed teen witnesses. In 2021, in Rochester, a nine-year-old Black girl was pepper-sprayed by police while she was handcuffed in the back of their car.

I've said it before, and I'll say it again: The only thing that separates me or any Black person from the headlines—and the countless violent incidents that we don't know of—is luck. It's pure luck. In 2001, in Walgreens, I didn't have the statistics, and I didn't need them. Somewhere inside, I already knew what I'd be facing.

My mother for sure already knew, and though I didn't realize it, she was preparing me. Before every playdate, Mom would say, "If someone says, 'Stop,' you stop." She'd remind me before going into a store, "Keep your hands out of your pockets and where they can be seen." If I asked when was the next time we were going into "Manha'an," she'd quickly correct me: "ManhaTTan." And finally, she'd say, "No matter what, just do what you have to do to make it home."

Preparation. She knew that a time would come where she wouldn't be there standing in the corner of a store, able to protect me with a hug. It was imperative that she give me the tools I'd need to survive as a Black child when moving through the world.

So, there he was. Standing at the end of the aisle. Waiting. Watching.

This wasn't a post-racial America, and I wasn't exempt from racism.

My instincts kicked in, instincts I didn't know I had. Black instincts. I smiled at the security guard, my way of saying, "I'se a friendly negro." I walked to him *slowly*, my way of saying, "I'se a polite negro." And as I walked, I could feel *his* instincts beginning to activate. I could see his eyes locked on me. I could see his chest puffing up. I could see his right hand twitching as it moved closer to his waist. It was important for me to speak. So I said with the best diction I could muster, "Excuse me, sir, do you know which aisle I can find the notebooks and pencils? I need new ones for school." My way of saying, "I'se an educated negro."

He looked at me, slightly confused but pleasantly surprised. His right hand stopped twitching. His arms rested by his side. His chest deflated. His eyes softened.

"Oh, yes, aisle five," he said.

"Thank you so much," I said with a bright smile. I made my way to aisle five, and he made his way back to the front door.

Luck.

Because, as a Black person, I know that the outcome could have been different. Who knows if there would have been a misunderstanding of my actions and presence? If there had been, who knows if I would have made it home? I have friends who had the same preparation, have the same instincts, and still managed to be staring down the barrel of a gun.

That day, I walked away unharmed...physically.

Swallowing your pride when you're in the wrong is one thing. Doing it when the other person is wrong is agony. Doing it as a means of safety from a person who is so, so wrong? That's just...I don't have the words.

My therapist encourages me to acknowledge when things are sad. It's hard for me, because it makes me feel too vulnerable, but yes, it's sad. Really fucking sad. And in the midst of that sadness is trauma. The kind that shapes a person. Changes a person. Changes a child.

Trauma like losing your innocence before your peers simply because of the color of your skin. Fighting for your safety without understanding that you're inside of a system built to lock you up or kill you. Having to be on alert and know how to assess every situation, because the white and non-Black *adults* around you will not protect you and may even harm you. (Some are even hoping to, in fact.) Not having the resources to unpack and process the daily mental aerobics of it all...trauma, trauma, trauma, trauma.

Perhaps getting me the Disney Channel was my mother's attempt to preserve as much of my innocence as possible. But being followed that afternoon was no match for Mickey Mouse and his cheerful gang of cartoon friends. Truthfully, there may have been plenty of other racist moments before that day, but there was no way for me to write off this interaction as anything other than what it was.

Recently, my husband and I started talking about having kids. I'm terrified over the prospect, not because I don't think I'd be a good parent or because I'm worried about how children will change the way our lives operate. I'm terrified because I know that there will come a moment in our Black children's lives where we'll have to *prepare* them. Where we'll have to stealthily chip away at their innocence while desperately trying to hold on to it for them. It's an impossible, unfair task. And that, too, is sad.

And yet maybe there's room for gray space here as well. Perhaps two things can be true. I find it sad, and yet I find myself in awe of children, especially Black children. I'm in awe of how they dust themselves off, cope, and survive. How they navigate the trenches of the adults around them and still end up being good, finding light in so much darkness. We'd probably call this resilience. You already know how I feel about that word, and I'm sad that Black children need so much of it. But it's how they survive.

After every racist or homophobic encounter I endured, I somehow still managed to make the honors list, laugh a lot, win school awards, foster meaningful friendships, and achieve so many goals. Still, that doesn't make the moment at Walgreens any less painful, particularly because it wasn't the last time I was followed, stared at, or taunted.

Ready to go deeper into the gray? I just said all of that stuff about resilience, but the shadow side of it is that I became hyper-aware of being perceived as a threat that day. An unasked-for reality came with the territory of being born in this skin, leading to my own fear of this skin. What if I was, in fact, a threat? What if I was dangerous?

So I overcorrected. I put away my Timbs. I pronounced every

hard consonant. I greeted every guard as soon as I walked into a store with a "Hello, sir, how are you today?" I didn't blame white supremacy or racism or bigotry for this need to perform certain societal norms and traffic in respectability politics. I was fourteen.

Every morning, I consider where I'm going and what to wear. This ritual is still rooted in my love for clothes and fashion, but there's this quiet lace of "make it home safely" that steers my choices. I just don't want to be followed, let alone find myself in a deadly altercation. I wish I could say it was a trauma from childhood that I should let go of, but we all know it's not. As I write this, I can't help but think about Ahmaud Arbery, who was simply jogging when he was hunted by murderous white men. I think about Breonna Taylor, who was *home* when she was gunned down.

So, ultimately, do the clothes even matter? Maybe sometimes. Or maybe it's just a psychological trick I learned to play on myself to calm my anxiety and fuel more resilience, a way for me to feel in control of something that I actually have no control over. I have no control over whether people are racist or biased in some other way or if they'll choose to act on their prejudices or not.

I hate even writing this, but I and many other Black folx just do our best not to provoke the hatred. It feels so fucked up to type "provoke," as if anyone is justified to kill a Black person for being Black. But that's what it feels like. We'll sometimes swallow our pride and slap on a smile because we gotta make it home. It's not fair, it's not right, but it's reality.

Historically, my Black Queer identity has been about proving I belong, and perhaps *that* is the case. Perhaps freedom comes from laying that burden down. But if I lay it down, what does that do to my safety? Do I dare find out?

The version of me you created in your head is not my responsibility.

—UNKNOWN

BLACK TRAUMA

It's my understanding that when you see me, fear overtakes you,

which ignites a necessity to stand your ground by putting me on the ground.

It's my understanding that when you see me, fear overtakes you,

which ignites a necessity to kill and explain later.

Or kill and get away with murder.

---

11. The Gorgeous Swan You Are

IF YOU COME VISIT OUR APARTMENT in Los Angeles, you'll see that my walls are covered in photos and artwork. I live for a gallery wall. In LA, interior design tends to be very clean and minimalistic, which photographs beautifully, but to me, this aesthetic always feels devoid of joy, warmth, and personality. I grew up in New York City, where everyone's apartments are an ode to where they've been, what they've seen, who they love, and what they value. So many brownstones or lofts overflow with color, irreplaceable artifacts, and anything that carries a story. I knew that when I was able to financially support myself, I wanted my apartment to reflect that same style.

By default, being financially stable in my industry a lot of times means being in more white spaces. When you spend as much time working with and around white people as I do, it's really easy to forget your values and be swept away by impostor syndrome. One of my ways to combat that was covering my walls in Black art, family photos, and treasured memorabilia. It's hard to pick my favorite piece, but one of the most important items hanging on my wall is a children's book called *The Ebony Duckling*. My mother read it to me all the time. As a rule, she made sure that the stories she read me before bedtime were filled with Black protagonists. One author I loved in particular, Fred Crump Jr., was known for taking famous fairy tales and retelling them with Black characters. Instead of *Jack and the Beanstalk*, it was *Jamako and the Beanstalk*. Instead of *Hansel and Gretel*, it was *Hakim and Grenita*. And instead of *The Ugly Duckling*, it was *The Ebony Duckling*.

The story begins with a brown-feathered mother duck waiting for her three eggs to hatch. Emerging from the first two eggs are adorable yellow baby ducklings. The third egg takes a bit longer to hatch, and when it does, out pops a dark black baby duckling who we come to know as the Ebony Duckling. Both the mother and father ducks insist that the Ebony Duckling couldn't be part of their family because he's "raggedy." They doubt he's even a duck, prompting them to mistreat him. Eventually the Ebony Duckling leaves to go on a search for a new family in hopes he can figure out what and who he is.

He tries to fit in with different bird families (geese, turkeys, and pheasants), but none will have him. Finally, he meets a majestic mother swan and her two swan babies, all with pristine white feathers. She tells the Ebony Duckling that he's not a duck but actually a swan, and offers to take care of him. There's a moment where the Ebony Duckling and his new swan family swim by his original duck family, and the story reads that the ducks "felt a little foolish not to have recognized this young prince amongst them." Obviously, the Ebony Duckling couldn't be happier to finally be accepted and have someone who cares for him, but he asks his new swan mother, "Why am I ebony?" The swan mother replies, "Ebony swans are precious and rare. When you grow up you will be the most beautiful bird on the farm." On the final page of the book is a gorgeous illustration of the Ebony Duckling as a grown and beautiful swan, and underneath the image it reads, "...indeed he was."

I wanted my mother to read me that story so often because I loved the pictures, but it was the story that really captured me. If I look back, the Ebony Duckling's experience of not belonging and being thought of as raggedy and unkempt was how I felt in the world. I've always had dark skin, darker than my classmates and friends, and I was made fun of for it. I can't count the amount of times lights would be turned off in a room and someone would yell out, "Where's Brandon?! Smile so we can see you." I'd always force a laugh so as not to kill the joy everyone else clearly got from the teasing.

I think my mother could sense my insecurity building in my middle school years, and one day she said to me, "Bran, you're so handsome." Me, with a pimply face, baggy jeans, and a plaid button-down over a white T-shirt. I simply shrugged. My mother, who in her youth also had her battles with not feeling beautiful in her dark skin, wouldn't let my nonchalance go unchecked. She stopped, looked me in my eyes, and said, "You know that you're handsome, right?"

In my head, I saw photos of Brad Pitt, Justin Timberlake, and whatever other white men the girls in my class were fawning over at the time. I didn't look or act anything like them, but I knew what my mother wanted to hear, so I mustered up a "Yes. I know." And she let it be. But I never saw evidence from the reaction of others that I was handsome or cute or attractive or beautiful.

I so desperately wanted to be beautiful.

My complexion was often a trigger, as it was the source not just of people's jokes but also of their rejection. At some point in college, I stopped posing for photos when I would go out at night (unless I was forced to or drunk) because the lighting was never right, and my white or light-skinned friends would look fabulous, while I— well, you could see my clothes. Later, with my acting career in full swing, I became the source of designers' complaints. The first television gig I ever booked, I'm barely lit, and it's criminal. There I am, talking amid an otherwise all-white group, and while everyone else in the scene is visible, I'm a dark amorphous blob. When you have countless experiences of being ridiculed or being made to feel like a burden because of your skin tone, it's easy to internalize that *you're* the problem.

Ismael, my bestie who I mentioned earlier, has the most stunning eyes and a brown complexion that, by comparison to me, makes him a "*light-skin nigga.*" There's a lot to unpack in that term, and before Ismael and I had the language to discuss it, we had a really tense moment during one of our drunk nights out. I don't remember how we got on the subject, but as Ismael recalls it, I looked at him venomously and said, "You so pretty. You light-skin nigga." Ismael played it cool and didn't react, knowing I was inebriated, but by my tone, it was clear there was anger and resentment that I had toward his complexion. It was something that I wasn't conscious of in a sober state, but with the help of a few margaritas, it became clear this was a thorn I needed to reckon with.

On top of never feeling beautiful, I was always seeing lighter-skinned Black people being propped up, valued, and fawned over. Be it on magazine covers or as TV heartthrobs or in prominent movie roles, the message was that light-skinned Black people were more attractive than their darker-skinned counterparts. It was easy to think perhaps I was gaslighting myself, but in 2014, there was a casting call for the movie *Straight Outta Compton* where they were searching for different types of Black women. They divided the search into four categories: A Girls, B Girls, C Girls, and D Girls. Below is the actual language used.

A GIRLS: These are the hottest of the hottest. Models. MUST have real hair—no extensions, very classy looking, great bodies. You can be black, white, asian, hispanic, mid eastern, or mixed race too. Age 18–30.

B GIRLS: These are fine girls, long natural hair, really nice bodies. Small waists, nice hips. You should be light-skinned. Beyoncé is a prototype here.

C GIRLS: These are African American girls, medium to light skinned with a weave.

D GIRLS: These are African American girls. Poor, not in good shape. Medium to dark skin tone.

Truly one of the most offensive casting calls I've ever seen, but clearly with such a reputable movie, casting company, and studio attached, the powers that be didn't think it was. They probably just thought they were being "factual" in their description.

But even with the prejudice directed at darker-skinned Black people, I now know that Ismael and many lighter-skinned Black folx have their own issues to contend with because they can feel the tension. They feel the anger and resentment from those of us who are darker while also having their Blackness questioned by both dark-skinned Black folx and white/non-Black folx. They constantly navigate taunts about how Black they are or aren't, both from within the community and outside it. It's the brilliant thing about white supremacy. The tools can be used by anybody, even me.

A couple years after that drunken night and the same year as that Compton casting breakdown, Ismael and I were watching *Oprah's Lifeclass*. (Like me, Ismael also prays at the altar of Mama O.) The episode we were watching featured spiritual teacher Iyanla Vanzant talking about colorism. Oprah defined it as "the light-skinned/dark-skinned prejudice where people of color discriminate against each other within their own race."

Ismael jumped up and said, "THAT! That's what you do to me!"

It knocked the wind out of me, because he was so right.

Oprah continued explaining: "It really boils down to the belief that the lighter your skin tone, the prettier you are. The smarter you are."

Iyanla chimed in, "The more valuable and worthy."

"True. And the easier you have it—that's the perception," Oprah finished.

It verbalized everything that I'd subconsciously felt and was subconsciously acting out in my relationship with Ismael. We both sat on the edge of the couch, watching studiously and hanging on every word, because for the first time, both of our experiences were being validated and articulated so clearly. Neither of us had realized the unconscious pain we had been causing the other by our little side comments or jokes. Neither of us was conscious of the ways in which we were trafficking in these tools of white supremacy.

That day on the couch watching Oprah and Iyanla was healing for my relationship with Ismael. From that day forward, we showed up for each other differently and championed each other intentionally. We weren't going to let white supremacy feed into our relationship any longer, and now that I had this awareness and language, I also vowed not to let it feed into my personal relationship with my dark skin. I was going to love my dark skin, even if the world categorized me as a "D Girl."

Easier said than done, baby, easier said than done.

I didn't realize how much I had deeply gravitated toward things that were white or white-passing, how much I was trained to reject my own skin and adopt a narrative that light-skinned Black people were better than me. It was second nature at this point, so trying to go against what I'd been taught felt unnatural. Comical, even. You should have seen me standing in the mirror late at night, repeating, "I am beautiful. I am beautiful. I am beautiful." But I would hear an internal voice respond, "You ain't beautiful! You ain't worthy! You ain't shit!"

I've used the word "beautiful" quite a few times now, and I'd like to take a moment to unpack and expand the definition. On a basic level, of course, I thought my desire to be beautiful was about looking like a model. But in reality, the pursuit was for something different. I once interviewed Nigerian American actor Chinaza Uche, a close friend of mine who I've known since we were eighteen, for my podcast *Black Folx*. Chinaza has an infectious smile, gentle spirit, enviable afro, and like me, deep dark skin.

On every episode, I would ask my guest one question to jump-start the hour-long conversation. The question I posed to Chinaza was "When was the first time you felt beautiful?" Chinaza paused, and as he pondered the question, he began to get emotional. He verbalized that it wasn't something he thought about. We both expressed how "beautiful" was a word that never felt like it could apply to us. The pain of that was palpable. Chinaza mused, "'Beautiful'—what does that word mean?...I think it's like [being] loved, celebrated, seen, accepted." (There's that word again: "accepted.") With that expansive definition, I later added that perhaps the real question is "When's the first time you felt valued?"

The Ebony Duckling wasn't yearning to be beautiful as in the sexiest bird on the farm. He yearned to be loved, celebrated, seen, and accepted. Growing up, I yearned to be loved, celebrated, seen, and accepted. And the only people I saw that happening to were white or light-skinned.

On the podcast, I told Chinaza that the first time I felt beautiful was in my mid-twenties, though I couldn't pinpoint the moment. Upon further reflection, maybe I wish it was in my twenties, though perhaps that's when I began the journey. The first time I actually felt beautiful was in 2019, a few months after turning thirty-two, when I was filming *Feel the Beat*. Like I said, Deco was the gay best friend, but I didn't want him to come off as a stereotypical Queer person, so as an actor, I did my homework to determine what would give this six-foot-one Black gay man the confidence to defy societal expectations in how he dresses.

I loved the idea that his confidence wasn't born from the rejection he could've faced for being Queer but rather out of the love and acceptance he experienced, something we don't often get to see in Queer stories. Then, after that conversation with my director where I shared that I could've grown up to be Deco under different circumstances, I had another thought: *Who would I be if society never got its hands on me? Would I be plagued with all this self-hate and doubt and anger and resentment, or would I feel beautiful?*

Who would I be if society never got its hands on me?

Something shifted in me once I posed that question. It's the question that I started this book with. I viscerally realized I'd been living my life for society and not for me. This quest to be physically beautiful was always dependent upon other people validating my beauty, but how could that ever happen if societal beauty standards are rooted in whiteness? And waiting for white people to validate me goes against everything I said I believed in. I was saying one thing, but there was this unchecked core belief actively informing my existence and contradicting my words. I knew I couldn't continue letting beauty standards that were never intended for me keep me from valuing myself.

After my exchange with the director, I went back to the hotel, sat in front of the window with the sunlight hitting my face, and took a selfie. I never take selfies, just like I'd rarely posed for photos. I always cringed at what I captured. But with this new revelation shaking my insides, I needed to take a photo. I set my phone up on the windowsill, set a timer on the camera, and posed wearing just a regular black T-shirt and a baseball cap over my durag. I quickly grabbed the phone to review the photos. An exhale escaped my mouth, and I said, "There you are." My little eyes, my big nose, my pillow-sized lips, the permanent wrinkle line across my forehead, and my dark ebony skin. For the first time in thirty-two years, I thought, *I'm beautiful.* And with that, the real journey to healing my relationship to my dark skin had begun.

One of the most important things I did for myself on this journey to healing that relationship was a photo shoot. My hesitation to take photos, even just when out with friends, revealed to me that there was an unconscious belief that I was an ugly ebony duckling. So I picked a photographer whose work included many Black subjects who were lit well. His name was Drew Blackwell, a gay man with an easy, warm demeanor.

The photo shoot was a transformative experience. It wasn't for headshots—which actors constantly have to do in an effort to get work—or social media, or for one of those Christmas-card updates people send out. This was strictly for *me*. There's a difference in how you experience life when your priority is taking care of yourself and your heart instead of trying to keep up with what everybody else is doing. And honestly, keeping up with everybody, especially those who you'll never look or be like, is the foundation upon which suffering is built.

The ABVs are always going to be a part of the human experience. I think the important thing to consider is who exactly you want to earn that acceptance, belonging, and validation from. Is it from folx who ain't trying to understand your walk of life and the pieces that shape you? Or is it from folx who value what you authentically bring to the table, who are openhearted and are engaged in their own life journey in a way that allows them to bring empathy, compassion, and support to their relationships?

I think so often we chase the wrong targets. We chase the folx who don't want anything to do with us unless we look a certain way or act a certain way. They show no interest until we make ourselves somehow useful to them. And my goodness, won't we contort our bodies into a stool for them to step on? Won't we tear our spirits to shreds for a scrap of their attention? And if you do get that attention, that acceptance, that belonging, that validation, it's not rooted in who you are, so now you have to keep up appearances. You have to keep up pretenses to continue getting those scraps. It's exhausting and not worth it. Spend that energy learning how to love and hype your own damn self, and then you can begin attracting the people who hold the fullness of you sacred.

If you don't love yourself—your skin tone, sexuality, body type, or any other part of your identity—then no matter how much anyone pours into you, it'll never be enough. There will always be an internal crack from which all that love will escape. You can't hold it if you don't see it for yourself. You can't hold what you don't believe. Other people's acceptance or validation of you should be a reaffirmation of what you've already affirmed for yourself.

Maybe over the years of my childhood, teenage years, and into my early thirties, there were people who valued my dark skin, but I missed it. There was no way for me to hold on to that possibility, because *I* didn't value my skin color. And standing in front of the mirror repeating, "I'm beautiful," "I'm worthy," "I'm valuable," over and over is a fine beginning, but without actions that match, the affirmations will not hold.

Your ability to thrive in your life is reliant upon you knowing that you are the shit. You don't have to know it every second of every day, but you do have to know it. You have to know you belong before anyone tells you so. Everyone's blueprint for loving themselves is inherently different. It's also a process that takes time and commitment. But I believe if you have an awareness of its necessity, you'll gradually begin to attract and create the tool that can forge your path there.

For starters, any person or place that wants to exclude you—fuck 'em. Remove yourself from the people and places that don't hold you in value. Unsubscribe, unfollow, block, or mute accounts and publications that trigger you. Surround yourself with images, books, and memorabilia that reflect your identity. Go where you're celebrated, not merely tolerated. Easier said than done, especially depending on your circumstances and location, but it's worth repeating: If you take nothing else away from this book, there is NOTHING wrong with you. You are enough. As you are, in this moment. As you sit there reading, or perhaps you're in your car or on the subway listening to the audiobook—however you're taking in these words, my angel, you are enough. The sooner you know that, the sooner you *believe* that, the sooner you can get about the business of thriving and growing into the gorgeous swan you are and have always been.

Stop breaking yourself down into
bite-sized pieces.
Stay whole and let them choke.
—UNKNOWN

YOUR HAIR, NOSE, AND SKIN ARE BEAUTIFUL

I mourn the countless days and nights of joy lost to the dreams of getting a nose job. The obsession with not letting my hair get "unruly." Hearing the names "monkey" and "darky" circling my peace. Attacking it with violent force. Staring in the mirror every chance I got and wishing I would see anything other than me.

We've been fed images our entire life that have told us our hair and nose and skin and bodies . . . and, and, and . . . were not enough. Were not normal, beautiful.

They lied to us.

That hair and that nose and that skin, they deserve your love. Your reverence.

It's the inheritance of your powerful ancestors.

AUTHOR'S NOTE: Therapy

At this point, you're probably like, "Brandon really don't give a fuck about when Author's Notes happen"—and you're very right, boo!

After all that I've discussed thus far, it feels important to take a moment and share some thoughts about one of the most life-changing things I've ever participated in: therapy.

"Ain't nothing Jesus can't handle" was something I heard over and over as a kid as a response to any conversations about therapy or mental health. "Give it to Jesus!" was another popular saying. Though that could be true, in my experience, Jesus was very quiet. My problems and issues were piling up, and the Holy Son wasn't so quick to reply to my queries. In His (capital "H") defense, there are a lot of people I'm sure He had to tend to, *and* I'm Queer, and apparently He ain't about that life. Perhaps He was purposely making me wait a little longer, but I needed support and needed it now.

While working as a barre instructor, I became close to one of my bosses, a very fit and artsy gay man named Todd. I loved Todd because he didn't do things by the book. He recognized that we instructors were individual humans who required different kinds of coaching or supervision, and he was happy to give it. His approach annoyed the higher-ups, but I loved it and used some of his teaching philosophy when I eventually stepped into a leadership role at the company. Because of how emotionally attuned he was, I thought he might know of a therapist. When I asked, his face lit up. He had the perfect person, a Queer Latine woman whose office was based in Chelsea a few blocks away from our flagship studio.

A few weeks later, I had my first session, and I've been with her ever since. As I write this, it's been around eight years that I've been in therapy. I will refrain from calling her my Jesus so as to prevent my grandmother from rolling in her grave or coming back to haunt me. Also, as tempting as it is to put a therapist on a pedestal because of how meaningfully they can impact your life, they're still human and should be regarded as such. But I couldn't write this book without talking about therapy and my therapist. It's how I'm able to unpack and make sense of the messy moments of my life.

For many in the Black community and even in some Queer spaces, therapy is a taboo. Many of us have been taught not to go telling family business to a stranger, and there's a perception that therapy is for rich white people with rich-white-people problems. Given the treacherous history of Black folx being used as experiments in the name of medicine, those fears are understandable. But also, times have shifted, and it's worth reexamining how we view therapy and mental health in general.

Our value has always been on being strong, not needing help, "sticking it out," "toughening up," being "resilient." Culturally, our productivity is valued far more than our sanity and sense of peace.

I believe that those of us from marginalized groups especially feel that we are only as good as what we do and can provide. We're hustlers to prove our worth. I for sure am. Growing up, I knew good grades, cleaning my room, being polite, or making a great joke would get me rewarded with validation, so I became a fiend for perfection. I craved it and still do.

I call myself a recovering perfectionist, not in jest or in any way to make light of addiction recovery, but because perfection is my addiction. Perfection has been one of the most destructive vices I've partaken in, and every day I have to remind myself to let it go. There have been times where perfectionism has left me in a depressive hole, where I would numb myself with too much food, alcohol, or sex.

Full transparency: Writing this book has been a struggle at times because of perfectionism. At times I'll catch myself obsessing over a comma placement before I've even completed the first sentence. I also find myself stressing over how someone reading this will perceive me and my stories. It's a constant inner dialogue reminding myself to just write, to just let the words land where they land. My first draft cannot and will not be good, and that's triggering, because I want the validation. I want to feel my worth.

A lot of times, our destructive behaviors are learned by way of family, because it's something our parents did, and their parents did, and their parents did. Intergenerational trauma. I believe therapy can be a tool to break those cycles. I believe there's much benefit to having someone in your life who's not a friend or family member but who can nonetheless give you a new perspective or ask thoughtful questions to help reframe the mess we've already experienced or the inevitable mess we're going to experience. If you think about it, life is hard, so why wouldn't we benefit from being in a relationship with someone who studies the human experience and psychology, who might be able to arm us with tools to navigate being alive? The right therapist can give you language to articulate the unformulated unconscious and bring it into consciousness. That's important because you can only heal what you're conscious of.

They say hurt people hurt people. They react instead of respond. I say a lot of hurt people don't even know they're hurting, because we numb ourselves so often with drugs, alcohol, food, shopping, sex, exercise, perfectionism, or other vices. Being able to articulate that hurt allows you to heal. Healing allows you to respond instead of react. To be clear, therapy isn't about putting yourself on some high horse as a master of emotions. But it does allow you to spend more time living this life in happiness because you know that when people react, they're reacting out of their own trauma that ain't got shit to do with you. You don't have to take their trauma on. You might be hurt, but you have the tools to process that hurt, communicate your boundaries, and heal, as opposed to passing that hurt on to someone you love.

If you are considering beginning therapy, please remember it's a relationship. I cohosted a podcast called *In Session*, with licensed clinical psychologist and one of my favorite humans, Dr. Janelle S. Peifer, all about mental health and season four of the HBO Max show *In Treatment* starring Uzo Aduba. Dr. Peifer likened meeting your therapist to dating, meaning you get to ask questions to make sure you and the therapist vibe. At any point, if you're no longer vibing with them, you get to leave. Therapists are human and have limitations. It's completely fair that you might need something they can't offer. Perhaps it's about identity—maybe you need a Black therapist, a woman therapist, a Queer therapist. Perhaps it's about style—maybe you like someone who gives you homework, who talks more or listens more. Whatever the case, you get to be in control of the experience. Don't think just because someone is a medical professional that you don't have the right to advocate for yourself.

I also want to acknowledge therapy isn't always affordable, even though it absolutely should be. There are resources out there that can help with costs, though it might require a little extra legwork. Still, the research will be worth it.

QUESTIONS YOU MIGHT CONSIDER ASKING A THERAPIST DURING YOUR FIRST SESSION

How does this work?

What is your therapeutic style or approach?

Have you ever had a patient who's dealt with [your reason for being there]?

What are your rules about communication outside of our sessions?

If I'm experiencing an emergency, is it okay to contact you? If not, what's the best resource available to me?

If you're nervous or have any specific concerns about the process, that's okay. It's actually helpful to share your concerns so that the therapist can talk you through it.

Author and poet Nayyirah Waheed so beautifully wrote, "If someone does not want me it is not the end of the world. But if I do not want me the world is nothing but endings." For me therapy was like a personal olive branch. A pathway to wanting myself again. A chance for my world and my most authentic life to finally begin.

Re-examine all you have been told in
school or church or in any book,
and dismiss whatever insults your soul.
—WALT WHITMAN

---

12. Pride and Joy

KNOW PEOPLE THINK I'M CRAZY when I tell them that most mornings I'm up at five a.m. My schedule is: Wake up at five, meditate and journal until six, make breakfast, get to the gym by seven, return home by eight thirty, walk/feed the dog, shower, change, and start work by nine thirty or ten. By the time I get to work or take a call, I've truly had a full day.

It wasn't always that way, though. When I was growing up, if I didn't have school, I would sleep past noon. Honestly, at heart, I've always been a night owl. In my teens and well into my twenties, I would stay up until two or three in the morning watching TV, or *Sister Act 2*, or writing some kind of poem or a random scene idea. I felt like my creative spirit came alive in those dark hours when the neighborhood and my household were deep in sleep. It was the time I felt I could really process and make sense of my life.

My grandmother was different. She would wake up at five a.m. (sometimes four) and lead prayer calls, which is basically a group of people on the phone praying together. Then she would make my breakfast and lunch and get me out of bed and ready for school by the time the bus came. Before she let me go out to the bus, she would hold my hands at the front door and pray over me.

"God's Holy Spirit goes before you, making safe, happy, and successful your way."

She'd tell me she loved me, kiss me on the cheek, and off I'd go. I would think she'd be cranky having to be up that early, but she loved it, and had a cheery and productive demeanor most mornings.

My mother, being a stage actress, had late nights performing, so she slept in most mornings. I'd usually see her after school until I became a preteen. My mother, up until that point, had experienced a certain level of success in her career but wanted more for herself and more for our lives. I think that newfound drive inspired her to double down and be more disciplined in her already structured schedule. Suddenly she was up at five a.m., doing yoga and meditating. With her new wake-up time, I now had both Grandma and Mom praying with me before I headed out to take the public bus. (I was a big kid now and could navigate public transportation by myself.) They were equally cheery and productive.

I didn't start waking up at five a.m. until my twenties, and it wasn't by choice. As a group fitness instructor, I had to teach six a.m. classes, but it was a requirement to be there fifteen minutes early. I'd get up as late as I could without missing the train and use the thirty-minute train ride from Hamilton Heights to Midtown to listen to Beyoncé, hoping it would help me plaster on a cheery disposition. It always worked, and clients would compliment me on how much energy I had so early. I'd smile and say, "It's because I love being with y'all so much." But really, it was Beyoncé.

Now, in my thirties, five a.m. is literally my favorite time of day. Don't worry, this chapter is not about convincing you to wake up that early. Honestly, it's less to do with the hour itself, and more to do with what happens at that hour.

As I mentioned, I grew up in a praying household. A religious household. My grandmother led those prayer calls because she had retired from being a minister shortly after I was born, but she never stopped loving the Lord.

The Lord, aka God, was strange to me. When I was old enough to learn about God, I learned: (1) God is a "Him," and (2) you have to capitalize the "H" when you talk about Him. (As a kid, I thought, *Wow, God must be pretty special to be the only one who gets a capital "H" mid-sentence.*)

My grandmother talked about this invisible figure with the highest reverence and made sure I knew he was always watching me. I once asked, "Like Santa?" She smiled gently and replied warmly, "No, like God."

Then I began learning about these rules God had in this book called the Bible that, as I understood it, wasn't written by Him but by some men. Still, it was His word, which we had to follow. This was overwhelming. An invisible man, authoring a book through the mouths of some (again, as I understood it) white men, filled with stories and rules by which we're supposed to live our lives, and if we don't—and this was the kicker—when we die, we go to a place called hell. (Are you keeping up with me?) Hell is ruled by a fallen angel by the name of Satan, who's the master of all sins and evildoing. If you sin, you must ask God for forgiveness so that when you die you can go to heaven. As a thirty-four-year-old, this is quite the load to process. As a six-year-old, this was terrifying. But I was assured that God was cool, and as long as I followed His rules and His will, Satan couldn't get ahold of me.

So I tried. I worked overtime to be good. To not sin or lie. To not do anything that would make Satan claim me for his own. I went to church with my grandmother every Sunday, and, though always bored, I stood for every song, read every scripture aloud, prayed, and repented, always knowing God (and the congregation) were watching me. I was a shoo-in to get into heaven!

And then puberty hit.

My guy friends became obsessed with swimsuit models and their boobs, while I preferred the boobs of Dwayne "The Rock" Johnson. I discovered the Rock because the guys in my class loved the WWF, and in an effort to fit in, I started watching as well. Muscular men sweating in Speedos, trying to pin each other down on the ground— a very easy sell. All the guys in class agreed the Rock was theee best wrestler. And I, too, agreed the Rock was theee best wrestler...who I wanted to wrestle me with his beautiful boobs, bulging biceps, and full lips. Obvi I never said that, but I thought it over and over, not making the connection that my desire for this man might be a clear indicator of my sexuality. (Teen denial was alive, chile!) And being in the thick of puberty, I also masturbated to him over and over.

I knew that thinking a guy was hot wasn't going to go over well with my male classmates, because they were vocal with their homophobia. But it wasn't until I saw a docuseries on MTV in which a kid was coming out of the closet that I understood the consequences of homosexuality.

As I remember, this seemingly nice boy realized he was gay and told his family, and they kicked him out of the house. I was devastated after watching. Again, at the time I didn't think that I was gay, but I also didn't think there was any reason a parent would kick their child out of the house, especially not for liking someone of the same sex. Was that really such an offense? I scurried to the kitchen where my grandmother and mother were preparing dinner and told them what I'd seen on TV.

"Would you ever kick me out?" I asked.

My grandmother, sitting at the table cutting vegetables, looked at me, puzzled. My mother, standing at the stove stirring a broth, looked at me with concern and asked, "Are you telling us you're gay?"

"No!" I immediately responded. "I just can't believe that family kicked their son out. Would you ever do that to me?"

"Of course not," my mother replied.

"But the Bible does tell us it's a sin," my grandmother added gently and lovingly. I wasn't sure if this was my grandmother's personal opinion or if she was just relaying what the Bible says. Either way, I felt my heart drop.

I may not have thought I was gay, but I was masturbating to men, which was "unnatural," according to some other church person I once heard speak on the subject. The last thing I would ever want to be was "unnatural," and I definitely didn't want to give Satan any reason to pull up.

I thought I could just ditch the Rock and change my masturbation material to something more acceptable. The internet was fairly new to me, and from talking to my classmates, I learned you could find what was known as "porno" on it. At night, when my grandmother and mother had fallen asleep and my inner night owl came to life, I logged on to the internet and began searching for "porno." I mean literally: I typed in "porno." An easy search led me to photos of women being penetrated by muscle-bound men. As you can guess, I had no interest in the women, and instead found myself entranced by the men. And then one of the websites provided a link for "gay porn."

My hands shook. "This is a sin," I kept repeating in a whisper. But I was aroused and curious. I clicked on "gay porn" and was taken to a page of links. No photos. Just a list of links. (Again, this was the '90s.) One caught my eye: Dino, the Italian Stallion. The name Dino was familiar because I was a big fan of *The Flintstones* growing up and, being that the show is set in the Stone Age, their version of a dog was a pet prosauropod-like dinosaur named Dino. In my mind, if I got caught on the site by my mom or grandma, I could say, "I thought it was a *Flintstones* website." Teenage logic is truly trash.

I clicked on the link and was taken to a very simple web page where I quickly learned that Dino was no dinosaur. He was a gorgeous, dark-haired bodybuilder with a clean-shaven face, pecs I wanted to bury my face in, and thighs that I wanted to be crushed between. I kept scrolling, keeping an ear out for the adults in the house in case they were to wake up. The photos were all from the same shoot—him shirtless on a beach, wearing a white Speedo. As I scrolled down the page, each picture got more explicit. Suddenly his white Speedo was wet and so was I. Scrolling some more, I soon got to the most important photo—Dino, standing naked on his beach towel, rock hard. And now I knew why he called himself a "stallion." I was overwhelmed and bursting through my pants. I believe the medical term is "dickmatized." Before I could process what was happening, I was eagerly masturbating, and as soon as I came, I felt a wave of deep guilt.

This is a sin.

I cleaned up, cleared the browser, and somberly went to my room to repent.

This became my cycle. I would resist for as long as possible but always fold. I'd look up Dino, masturbate, repent. I tried desperately to stop, but then all I could see were shirtless muscled men everywhere. They were on TV, in magazines, on the street. I'd imagine what they looked like naked and then masturbate to those images in my head late at night, followed by an hour of repenting, praying, crying—all in fear. I'd print out photos for safekeeping, and then cry as I tore them to shreds after orgasm. My attraction wasn't going away.

I felt so much shame and disgust for myself from age thirteen until I came out in my twenties. That's a long time to be silently suffering over something that I would eventually learn wasn't bad, wrong, or a sin. It was a long time to feel like this invisible man had forsaken me by not taking this gayness away.

Once I started college, I stopped going to church. Instead I spent my Sundays nursing hangovers and wincing at embarrassing flashbacks from the night before. But even though I didn't miss church, I missed something. I missed the act of prayer, the act of acknowledging blessings and universal alignment.

Then I remembered my years of watching *The Oprah Winfrey Show*. She would always talk about spirit, noting that religion and spirituality aren't the same. In my experience with religion, specifically Christianity, there were a lot of rules laced with judgment and fear meant to control those of us who didn't stay in line. But just because I chose not to go to church didn't mean I couldn't have my spirit and develop my own relationship to God. For me, "God" is another way of saying "the universe," "energy," or even "good vibes." I had to unlearn the idea of a mysterious and invisible (white) father figure in the clouds. I had to unlearn the red demonic ruler of the underworld. I had to ground myself inside the reality of my life. What are my values? What are my beliefs? Kindness. Love. Joy. Inclusivity. Human connection. Vulnerability. Laughter. Why be so focused on who someone sleeps with when you can spend your time focused on kindness, love, joy, inclusivity, human connection, vulnerability, and laughter? When I began to shift my focus to these values in my twenties, my heart began to breathe.

Make no mistake: This shift happened gradually. Like anything, it takes time to unlearn things that make us feel shame and transition our new ideas and perspectives into core beliefs. It took until my mid-twenties for me not to feel guilty over not attending church. It took until my late twenties to verbalize my shift. And in my early thirties, I was able to own my spirituality without needing to justify it with traditional religious symbols like church or the Bible. Spirituality in and of itself is enough. This was a major break from the traditional teachings of my grandmother, and I learned to be okay with that.

Over the years in that journey to spiritual enough-ness, I would feel there wasn't anything wrong with me. I could see those rules in the Bible for what they were—words written and interpreted by men. Humans with agendas. Humans with a taste for power and a need for control. Humans who didn't know me, my journey, or my heart. There were plenty of folx who could recite Bible verses (never a strong suit of mine), but then you'd hear that they were cheating on their wife or abusing their kids or stealing from the church. Knowing Bible verses, going to prayer meetings, and never missing a Sunday service does not make one a good human. So why was I concerned by what Bible-toting folx thought about me? Why was I not concerned about what I thought of myself?

To be clear, I have no problem with Christianity, or any religion for that matter. Whatever practice brings out the best version of a person is beautiful. My relationship with Christianity was a harmful one, but I know plenty of Queer Christians who've found a way to navigate the church without compromising the integrity of their identity.

I chose to put the Bible aside and find new teachers and thought leaders and artists, some of whom were Christian. What I began to do was create a spiritual practice tailored to me, one that fit me, instead of adopting something just because I was raised to believe it. We're raised to believe a lot of things, but no one has ever been raised by a perfect human in a perfect world, so it's beyond okay to get curious, to question what you've been taught and decide if it really aligns with who you are and the life you want to lead.

The reality is, none of us knows what happens when we die, so to live solely by the confines of something dictated by when you die seems like not the best use of this life. I'm nice to people not because I don't want to go to hell. I'm nice to people because it feels good. If you're working on building your spirituality—which I highly recommend—you can find it anywhere. My husband finds it on long hikes, camping trips, and beach days. I find it in morning meditations, journaling, and watching YouTube videos of Whitney Houston or Beyoncé. I mean babe, Whitney's voice, Beyoncé's... everything—that shit is spiritual!

That said, I understand why people cling to religion as it is. I understand why people live solely by the confines of something dictated by what's supposed to happen when you die...because people die.

I was feeling pretty good about my decision to stay away from church and keeping my Bible on the shelf until it was clear that my grandmother was coming to her last days. Though I became ambivalent about inheriting her religious beliefs because of the impact Christianity had on my sexuality, I nonetheless deeply loved this woman. She'd fallen sick again, and we were told that she could still live, but that it would be time to put her in hospice. I'd never heard the term before. I guess people don't generally talk about hospice care, because naturally it's a devastating topic. (If you're unfamiliar, hospice care is health care that caters to patients who are terminally ill. If someone you know or love enters hospice, they're in their final days.) Essentially, Grandma would either die in the hospital that week or in hospice shortly after.

I was born at 8:08 p.m. on May 20, 1987, at Booth Memorial Hospital in East Elmhurst, Queens. The story I've always been told is that my grandmother was in the middle of leading a prayer meeting or some kind of function at the church and had to leave early when word got to her that my mother was in labor. My nursery and eventual bedroom was down the hall from my grandmother's room. My mother's bedroom was in between us. As I got older, my mother moved out of the house, but so as not to interrupt my schooling, I stayed with Grandma.

I didn't understand it while she was alive, but I was my grandmother's pride and joy, though I'll probably never fully know what that phrase means until I have grandkids of my own. Simply put, I was her favorite. Her world. Some of my cousins and even my mother would commiserate about how strict my grandmother was with them growing up, yet with me she was putty. Sure, she had rules, and she certainly didn't play games when it came to respect and responsibilities. But she was always available for a hug and gave the best ones. She was always excited to tuck me in and always ready to brag about her "smart, talented, handsome grandson." We had an inexplicable bond during my childhood that became strained in my teenage years.

Both of us were coping with the challenges of getting older. I dived deep into my teenage rebellion phase, with college on the way, all while trying to keep a lid on my burgeoning Queerness. And she reckoned with the physical, emotional, and psychological deteriorations related to aging.

Before it was a trendy thing to say on social media, Grandma was the definition of a "boss queen." The sixth of seven children and the first to immigrate from Trinidad to America, she managed to do everything she was told she couldn't do as a Black woman: Get her green card, raise her daughter by herself, buy a house by herself, change careers, run churches and a school, do missionary work in Tanzania, and be an instrumental, inspiring figure in so many people's lives. With her never-ending list of personal and professional accomplishments, most of which took place before I was even a thought in my mother's brain, it was hard for her to slow down. She didn't want to, but her body decreed otherwise.

All my life, she had been this larger-than-life presence, and suddenly I was taller than her. All my life, I knew her to be able to recite every single phone number in her contacts book from memory, also doing all kinds of crazy math without using a calculator or even writing anything down. But suddenly she was blanking on my name.

Suddenly she was hunching over and using a cane. Suddenly there were more doctor visits, more tests to run, and a wheelchair. And then she was in a nursing home. This person who used to pick me up onto her hip, who used to let me sleep in her bed even when everyone said I was too old, who used to stand at the front door and pray over me before sending me off to school, now barely recognized me.

I didn't have the language or the resources to process what I was witnessing, the grief that I was experiencing. My mother didn't either. She was very much in fix-it caretaker mode. Understandably, she only had the capacity to take care of Grandma. She wasn't really taking care of her own emotions, let alone mine.

By the time Grandma was in the phase of asking about the whereabouts of her brothers, most of whom had been dead for years and years, I was about nineteen or twenty. Because of my school schedule, I only saw her on holidays. Or so I told myself. Realistically, with her being about ninety minutes away from campus, I'm sure I could have gone to a couple fewer parties and made time to get to her, but avoidance was my defense of choice. I'd also come out of the closet at that time and was afraid to tell her, petrified that my mere existence was a betrayal of the religious beliefs she held dear.

When I did see her, her body and mind appeared weaker and weaker. At a certain point, we stopped taking her to holiday functions because the journey was just too much for her and us. At a certain point, she stopped talking very much. She was just kind of there.

When I was twenty-three and living with Kevin, I got the call from my mother about Grandma being in the hospital and the possibility of hospice care. I went to the hospital immediately to see Grandma laid up in bed, not really conscious, as my mother was doing her best to hold it together. New visitors continually arrived to see Grandma. As I stood in the hallway, watching familiar faces step off the elevator and into Grandma's room, I realized that things were about to change. The matriarch of our family was about to complete her journey. I didn't know what that meant for me, nor did I care. I just wanted her to be okay, and if that meant dying, then I just wanted it to be painless. I hadn't been able to hold a cohesive conversation with my grandmother in a couple of years, but I knew the sharp-witted, feisty, strong, loving grandmother who raised me was somewhere still inside that body. I also knew she was tired.

For two days, my mother played host to the many people who wanted to visit Grandma in the hospital. There were tears at times, and there was uproarious laughter, especially when one of her childhood friends visited. I call her Auntie Cherryl. She'd just experienced the loss of her own mother not too long before and was well versed in how to take care of my mother's complicated emotions. She knew that my mother couldn't be my mother right now. She needed to be a daughter. Auntie Cherryl also knew how to take care of me, and we welcomed the joy she brought.

Almost in the blink of an eye, it was nighttime. Most visitors had left, and my mother was in the hallway. It was the first time in two days that I had a moment to be alone with Grandma. The first time I really needed heaven to be real. The first time I understood why she and so many others clung to the Bible. The Bible may have some harmful flaws, but it also has answers and explanations. Whether they're correct or not is irrelevant. They're comforting. They help make sense of the discomfiting moments that speak to our mortality.

Her dying made no sense. It felt unfair. She was such an incredible and generous and good human. Why should she have to go? And where was she going?

I sat on her bed, the same way she'd sat on mine every night growing up. I adjusted her blanket, tucking her in the same way she'd tucked me in every night. I wanted to pull her into my arms but didn't want to disturb the tubes that were attached to her body. So instead I took her hand. My mother was adamant about lotioning them, so they were softer than ever. When I was younger, I loved the bigness of her hands and the little lines on the side of her palms that went up and around her thumb. But now her hands rested delicately in the bigness of mine.

I looked at her, savoring the moment. I was coming back tomorrow, but I wasn't sure if I'd get more alone time like this. Should something happen while Mom was out of the room and I'd been the one who asked her to leave, I would never forgive myself. But this was organic. I wanted to believe God created this little private moment for my grandmother and her pride and joy.

While sitting there, I remembered a play I'd read maybe a month or so prior called *Carnival Round the Central Figure* by Diana Amsterdam. In it, one of the characters is terminally ill and lying in a hospital bed. The main character says something about how sometimes people need permission to leave. To transition. To die. And so she gives that to him. When I read that, I remembered thinking how important it is to liberate someone from their suffering if you're able to. Love liberates. I didn't know if it was true that someone dying can hear you even if they're not conscious, but I knew Grandma was suffering in her fight to hold on. So I gave it a shot.

I don't remember everything I said, but I know that I squeezed her hand and whispered something like:

I love you. We are going to be fine. You've done enough,
and we are going to be fine. You did it. You don't have to
fight anymore. If you're ready, I promise we'll be okay.
We are in God's hands. He has us, and He has you. I love
you. I love you so much, and I promise we're going to
be fine. I love you. God's Holy Spirit goes before you,
making safe, happy, and successful your way.

I kissed her on the cheek and went back out into the hallway
to find my mother. She seemed to be in better spirits, though still
exhausted. Grandma was stable, and transitioning her to hospice
was looking like a possibility. Mom decided she would sleep at
home that night. She gave Grandma a kiss, and then, with my arm
around her shoulder, Mom and I got into the elevator.

The next morning, I woke up to a voicemail from my mother.
The time stamp was something like four thirty in the morning. I
knew before I listened that Grandma was gone. It's not lost on me
that she passed in the early hours when she used to have her prayer
calls. Her favorite time of day.

I never told Grandma I was gay, and I don't know if there's a
heaven or hell. But even though I don't claim religion, it still com-
forts me to think that Grandma is in heaven and that one day I'll
be there, too. And I think that's okay. I think it's okay to take the
pieces of religion that work for you, that comfort you, leaving
behind anything that causes harm and suffering. So, no, I haven't
opened a Bible or been to church in years. Yes, I love gospel music
and listening to sermons on YouTube. I interpret the messages in
a meaningful way that feeds my spirituality without feeling like

I have to be chained and controlled by the "rules." And every now and then, I imagine going to heaven and reuniting with my grandma. I imagine her introducing me to all the people I never got to meet in our family. I imagine getting to talk to her about love and work and dreams in ways that my six-year-old self wasn't capable of understanding and my sixteen-year-old self wasn't ready to.

In heaven, I imagine her saying, *I'm sorry I thought being gay was a sin. I'm sorry you weren't ever able to tell me you were Queer. But I see you now. And I love you as you are. And I'm so proud of you. You are my pride and joy.*

Keep looking up and pray.

—GRANDMA

AUTHOR'S NOTE: Ancestors

There's this balancing of reality and dreams that I find myself trying to hold space for. I have big dreams for my life, for my career, for my community, for my world. At the same time, I have to recognize the reality of the world that doesn't allow Black folx, Queer folx, or anyone who doesn't fit perfectly into a pretty cis-het white box the opportunity to make those dreams come fully to fruition. I think about my ancestors who may have wanted to write a book, or start a business, or be openly gay, but the reality of the world literally didn't allow them to do that. But they still lived, hopefully as close to authentically as possible, even if it had to be in the shadows.

Some of those ancestors found a way to push the needle forward. My family and I know the names of a few, but obviously there are so many who lived and pushed and fought and strived, and we'll never know anything about them. But they made space for those who were to come. And now I sit here writing my first book, under the first Black-led imprint of a very respected publishing house, and I can't help but think about my ancestors. I can't help but think about my great-grandmother and great-grandfather on my mother's side. I have a picture of each of them in one of those small double frames that now lives on my desk, beside a picture of me and my grandmother from before I cut off my locs. Both photos of my great-grandparents are black-and-white, almost full-body shots, somewhere in Trinidad. I didn't know their names until after my grandmother passed away and it was written in her eulogy. Grandma always just called them Mama and Papa.

My great-grandmother was named Juliana Joseph. In the photo she stands in front of a big tree, wearing a dress that looks a little too big in the shoulders and an apron. Her face is gentle, stoic. She looks strong but tired. It feels as though there are at least a thousand other things she should be doing besides taking this photo, yet here she is, slightly annoyed. You can tell she gets shit done, which makes sense, because my grandmother ran shit. I can kind of see my grandmother's face in hers. I wish I could see my face, but I don't quite. Yet I feel like if I were to meet her in person, I'd know that we were family. I'd know that I belonged to her.

My great-grandfather Alexander Paul stands in front of a tree as well—a different one than Juliana. He's dressed impeccably in a suit and tie with a fedora. His pants have a crisp pleat that makes him look very distinguished. He's tall and lean with a stoic face. His bone structure lets you know he was probably a beautiful young man. But there's also something hard about him. Or hardened.

Something about his cheeks reminds me of my mother. Something about his hands reminds me of my own.

Both photos, side by side, exude tradition, as though there were expectations and roles they both had to abide by and did. Were they happy? Perhaps. Were they funny and warm people? Perhaps. But these photos certainly don't tell that story. They do tell me that my great-grandparents were hard workers. And the few times I heard my grandmother speak about them, she lit up, so I imagine they were good people. They did right.

Juliana and Alexander had seven children, and my grandmother Virginia was the sixth born. I don't think Juliana or Alexander had the space to dream about a great-grandchild, and I can't imagine they ever dreamed of one like me. I wonder if they would marvel at my willingness to abandon the world's expectations of me or if they'd be disappointed that I didn't honor tradition. I wonder what Juliana wanted, and if Alexander was it. I wonder what Alexander wanted, and if Juliana was it. I don't question whether or not they were great parents, even great spouses, but were they ever given the space to ask themselves, "What do I want?" And if they had the awareness to ask that question—the space to ask that question—was there a world in which they could actually pursue their dreams?

I fight hard to live my life because so many couldn't.

I'm openly gay because so many couldn't be.

I'm open about my gender identity because so many couldn't be.

I ask myself, "What do I want?" often, because so many couldn't.

I pursue my dreams because so many couldn't, but they sacrificed so that I could.

I'll never know Juliana and Alexander in the flesh of life, but in its spirit, I honor them.

I honor every ancestor whose name I don't know, who cleared a path, knowingly or not.

And one day I'll be someone's ancestor, so I'll live as free as I can so they can live freer. So they can expand the definition of free beyond anything I could dream.

13. **Three-Fifths**

RYING TO FIGURE OUT WHO I was before society got its hands on me. Before I was conditioned. Before I was trained to follow a rule book that at one point considered me three-fifths a person. Might still consider me three-fifths a person.

Who would I be if your validation and your acceptance didn't matter?

Who would I be if my livelihood didn't depend on your ability to label me?

Who would I be if I escaped the plantation of your psyche?

Flawed.

Full.

Brandon Kyle Goodman

Human.

Me.

14. **You Gotta Be You**

MUCH LIKE WHEN I WAS writing my introduction, I'm sitting here staring at my computer, thinking about how I want to end this book. What I want my final words to be. I've written a few versions of the final chapter already, and I'm unsatisfied by them all. I began heavily debating not writing one, because it feels daunting. In truth, it's my perfectionism taking hold, an impassioned desire to create the "perfect" ending. I've been pretty good about managing it through most of the writing process, but with only a few days before I have to turn my manuscript in, my inner perfectionist is raring their anal-retentive, controlling, critical, high-expectations-having head.

My mother would always tell me that if I find myself caught up in my own bullshit, then I should pour myself into service of others, so if you don't mind, I'm going to stop thinking about the stories I want to tell and the best way to complete this book, and instead think about you.

As you can imagine, when I began writing, my editor, Krishan, a brilliant Black woman who never minces her words and compassionately advocates for excellence, asked me who I wanted to read this book. *Who is this book for?* I expressed that I wanted to write a book for that Black or POC Queer person navigating the pieces of their identity. I wanted to share the ways in which I've brought those pieces together instead of compartmentalizing them. I wanted to articulate some of my more challenging experiences so that they would know they're not alone and they're not gaslighting themselves. I wanted to show how it's possible to turn trauma and pain into a powerful source of compassion and love, especially love of self. I wanted them to know that thriving is their birthright. That advocating for their life is their birthright. Joy, support, and being authentically themselves are their birthright. Healing and growth are their birthright.

Most importantly, I wanted them to know they are enough. I wanted everyone else who might read this book to also know those things, in addition to understanding that even though we may have different identities from one another, we're all human. As the Roman philosopher Terence said, "I am a human being, and thus nothing human is alien to me." We all want the same thing in this life. Acceptance. Belonging. Validation. To love and to be loved.

The perfectionist in me is stressing, because those are big goals, and I'll never have control over how this book impacts you. But what I do have control over are my final words to you, which may not be perfect but will be intentional.

Dear Reader or Listener,

At one point I thought I would end this book by writing a letter to my younger self filled with all the things I wish someone had said to me growing up. And while that would be a meaningful exercise personally, my younger self is never going to read this book, unless one of these billionaires is working on some freaky technology we don't know about. But *you're* reading it, so I think it's more important to say those things to you.

You, my love, are something special. I know it doesn't always feel that way. I know the world and maybe even your family don't always make you feel that way. I know there are a million voices swirling in your head questioning the validity of your existence. I know that you've experienced pain that felt crushing. I know you've experienced trauma that was crushing. I know you've cried or screamed or gone numb because it was too much. Life. That there were moments where you wondered if it was even worth it. Life.

When I was twelve years old, unable to bear the constant taunting I experienced from my classmates over my femininity, I wrapped my church tie around my neck, went into my closet, and tied the other end on the higher rod while standing on a little crate. I had a note on my desk written to my mom, grandma, and the kids at school. I stepped off the crate, and the rod broke immediately.

I ended up on the floor, sitting in a pile of clothes, alive and terrified. My mother heard the noise and yelled from downstairs, "What was that?"

"I fell," I hollered back. But she wasn't satisfied with the answer. Mother's intuition, perhaps. As I heard her making her way up the stairs to my room, I quickly untied myself, closed my closet door, grabbed a textbook, and sat at my desk. My mother opened the door and I plastered on a smile. She examined the room but never went into the closet. Once she determined everything was okay, she sternly told me to be careful and get my homework done. And I did. I never told her or anyone about the attempt to take my life. About my pain. There didn't seem to be space for it. And even if there was, I didn't have the language to describe my torment.

Now I can articulate that the pain I felt was because I didn't fit the boxes that were set up for me. I didn't fit the ideals or expectations placed on me. I was told:

"You gotta be masculine."

"You gotta be straight."

"You gotta be more Black."

"You gotta be less Black."

"You gotta be the man."

"You gotta be a strong Black man."

"You gotta be smarter."

"You gotta be successful."

"You gotta be articulate."

"You gotta be measured."

"You gotta be religious."

"You gotta be obedient."

"You gotta be likable."

"You gotta be well dressed."

"You gotta be well mannered."

"You gotta be nonthreatening."

"You gotta be excellent."

"You gotta be twice as good."

"You gotta be five steps ahead."

"You gotta be what your job tells you to be."

"You gotta be what your family tells you to be."

"You gotta be what society tells you to be."

There was so much emphasis on what I "should" be and no honoring of who I was. I did my best to be those things, but no matter how hard I tried, something was always off, which kept a target on my back. The feeling of shame for not being "normal" was nauseating. Debilitating. But pain don't have to last forever, which is why I hope when *you* wake up every morning, you get about the business of learning to love who you are and challenge what you may have been taught to believe about your identity. I hope you hold yourself sacred.

It may not be easy. There are so many systems and people committed to keeping you in your place and putting you in your box, but there are also people and communities who want to see you expand. Soar. Make sure you're committed to finding these people.

Loving yourself doesn't mean there won't be obstacles or setbacks, but we get through things. You get through things. You're here, reading this book, despite what you've gone through or are going through. You're here. How many times have you been counted out, underestimated, rejected? And you're still here. That's not a small thing, babe. The evidence of your life proves time and time again that you're tough. A warrior. That you belong here.

I can't take your pain away. I can't protect you from trauma. But I can remind you of your strength. And I'm not just talking about the strength to persevere. I'm talking about the strength to cry, to rest, to ask for help. The strength to be honest with yourself. The strength to walk away from the things and people who aren't good for you no matter how much you want them to be.

I'm so proud of you. So proud of who you are and who you're becoming. I also know you want more. You have ambitions, dreams, and desires. And you deserve them all, but as my Jamaican godmother, Auntie Vernice, said to me once, "When you find yourself comparing yourself to others, wake up!"

One of the most important things you can do every single day that I promise will quiet voices of comparison and help you root for yourself is express gratitude. Every morning in my journal, I try to write down at least three things I'm grateful for. Sometimes I'll write ten. If you write one, that's fine!

It can be as simple as *I'm grateful to be alive* or *I'm grateful for the breath in my body.* It can be as fluffy as *I'm grateful for that delicious slice of pizza I had last night* or *I'm grateful for the way* Real Housewives of Atlanta *keeps me laughing.* It can be as profound as *I'm grateful for my heart that continues to expand with love and trust for who I am. I'm grateful for my challenges that have deepened my well of empathy for all whom I encounter.*

Nothing is too big or small, too frivolous or abstract to be grateful for.

We won't always have our lives in perfect working order. That's just part of being human. It's what you do with the mess that matters. Resilience may be a fine and necessary survival mechanism, but don't be afraid to get M.E.S.S.Y. and go after your healing. (Remember: **M**ake space to reflect curiously. **E**asy on the judgment. **S**urrender the things you can't change. **S**ave the lessons you can move forward with. **Y**our healing and growth are your birthright.) So "give up hope that the past could have been any different," and hold space for what is right now.

They say in marketing that a consumer needs to hear a message seven times before they'll take action to buy a product or service.

I've lost count of how many times I've stated some version of the following, but here it is one last time...

If you remember nothing else that I've written,
please remember that you matter.
You are necessary.
You are worthy.
You are enough exactly as you are.
And in case you haven't heard it yet today, you are
so deeply loved, AND there's nothing "you gotta be"
except who you really are.
I love you,
BKG

Acknowledgments

B ABY, WRITING A BOOK TAKES a village of support! This has been a journey unlike anything I could have ever imagined for myself. One that has challenged me, expanded me, pissed me off, rattled me, delighted me, shocked me, and fulfilled me. I have laughed, wept, screamed, procrastinated, rolled my eyes, and taken enormous cleansing breaths. That said, I want to thank all the people who held my hand through the writing process, and also those who have held and continue to hold my heart during this process of being a human.

My Teachers:

Ellen Barber, Monica Robbins, Nini Selwanes, Donna Beckles, Marisa Ortega, Madame Nathalie, Casey and Libbie Zimmer, Katie Bull, Peggy Pettitt, Paul Binnerts, and Rosemary Quinn—you protected me in spaces that were challenging for my Black

Queerness to exist. You made me feel seen, special, and valued. You gave me tools to express myself. You encouraged me and believed in my gifts. You nurtured my heart. You loved me before I knew how to love myself. Thank you.

My Family:

Mom and Grandma—you inspired me beyond words by following your dreams. You did what others said was impossible with grace, integrity, compassion, and love. You broke down walls and barriers and gave me a blueprint for believing in one's self. You modeled strength and fortitude for me. You instilled in me the importance of kindness and goodness. You showed me how to be a good person. You showed me how to be a good friend. You showed me how to be good to myself. You taught me that growth and evolution is a process that should never end. You believed in me before anyone else did. You gave me my wings and regardless of everything else, I stand on your shoulders. For that, I am forever grateful.

My Godparents:

Uncle Ronnie, Auntie Smoochie, Uncle Dudley, Auntie Biti, Auntie Valsie, Auntie Vernice, Auntie Cherryl, Uncle Barry, Auntie Phyllis, Uncle Yvans, Uncle Lamont—some of you my mother picked to give that title to, and others I picked. All of you filled in where my blood could not. You gave me guidance, support, and love. You shared your wisdom and held my heart in some of the darkest moments, always believing I would get through. You are my Earthly angels. My first experience with chosen family. My backbone. My protectors. Thank you for loving me as your own.

My Chosen Family:

Ruth Morin, thank you for reading every single chapter, giving me your thoughtful feedback, creating space for challenging and emotional conversations, and for holding the very raw versions of this manuscript sacredly. I could not have gotten through this process without your unwavering and unconditional love, support, and care.

Ismael Cruz Cordova, Fernando Contreras, Cherrye Davis, Mackenzie Rose Cook, Traci Thomas, Chelsea Gentry, Kyle June Williams, Michael Medico, Lisa Bierman, nicHi douglas, Chinaza Uche, Devere Rogers, Dominique Toney, Lyo Reneau, Carlis Shane Clark, Stacy Osei-Kuffour, Kelli J. Bartlett, Kirk Vaclavik, Mycah Hogan, Brittany Kagan, Meaghan Oppenheimer, Tom Ellis, Adam Wasserman, Sasha Sagan, Kendyl Wright, Jacob Tobia, Dr. Janelle Peifer, and the rest of my chosen family—thank you for loving me as I am. For showing me that there's nothing wrong with how I live and love. For exemplifying unconditional love. For the deep belly laughs, the ugly cries, the expansive conversations, late brunches, and safety net. My ability to take big chances on myself, like writing this book, is because I know that no matter what happens, I have your love to catch me. You reflect back to me time and time again that I am enough. I wish that every person would know what it is to have a tribe like you. To have a love like yours. Being loved by you is truly one of the greatest privileges and honors of my lifetime. Thank you for letting me love you the same.

My Colleagues:

Nick Kroll, Andrew Goldberg, Mark Levin, Jennifer Flackett, Kelly Galuska, Kelsey Cressman, Mitra Jouhari, and everyone else at *Big Mouth* and *Human Resources* who were patient, flexible, and supportive with me as I wrote this book. Thank you for making me a better writer and for showing me how to share the scariest parts of my existence with humor, heart, compassion, and grace.

My Reps:

Tatiana Sarah, thank you for being more than a manager. For seeing the vision I have for myself and never questioning it, but instead jumping on board and helping me bring it into fruition. There's no one I trust more to cut the brakes with.

Derek Kroeger, Danielle Schoenberg, Adam Van Dusen, Joe Veltre, Jordyn Palos, Jade Wiselogle, the Gersh Agency, and the William Morris Endeavor Agency—thank y'all for always having my back and going to the mat for me. You've helped me shape a career beyond my imagination, and the little BKG who used to write poems at the bottom of their grandmother's staircase is forever grateful.

My Book Team: Krishan Trotman, Clarence Angelo, Amina Iro, Kathryn Gordon, Abimael Ayala-Oquendo—thank you for giving me the keys to tell my story. For championing me. For reassuring me. For responding to my panic emails with kindness and graciousness. For reminding me of the bigger picture when my fears got the best of me. For asking the thoughtful questions, and helping me say exactly what I've always wanted to say. What I've always needed to say.

My Therapist:

Eight years and counting! This book would not exist if it weren't for the ways in which you've helped me to reflect on and make sense of my life. You have pushed me harder than anyone to advocate for myself. You have called me on my bullshit. Held space for tears. Restored my faith in myself and taught me how to finally love myself. You have allowed me to be messy, never judging my missteps, and helped me create a path to healing. When I wasn't able to afford you, you adjusted your rate, recognizing the dark hole I was quickly sinking into. Being able to rely on you through the ups and downs has saved me time and time again. Thank you!

My Heart:

Matthew Raymond-Goodman—I need to write a whole other book to properly thank you. More than my husband, you are my partner. You have never seen me as your other half, but as a whole person. You've made space for my past, held me in the present, and dreamed with me about our future. You've been the definition of patient. You've been my light in so much darkness. You've been my hope. You've been the beat to my heart. I didn't know love could keep growing like this. I didn't know safety could feel this good. You've given my life the opportunity to stop fighting. You've allowed me to just be myself. Fully. Boldly. Unapologetically. You've loved every piece of me. The good, the bad, the gray. Never shaken, never stirred, never scurred. You show up for me. To know a love like yours is a treasure. To have a love like yours is spiritual. I wish my grandmother could have met you. I fear she'd like you better and honestly, same. I love you puzzle piece babe. Forever and ever.

You:

The reader/listener—thank you for holding my stories. For being. For existing. For loving. Rooting for you always.